1(......

for *Practicing*
PYTHON

A set of exercises with different levels
of complexity:
Beginner, Intermediate, Advanced

Laurentine K.Masson

Table of contents

Exercise 1

Write a sequence of Python instructions to declare 3 variables **a, b**, and **c**, assigning them the values **1**, **'France'**, and **36.2** respectively, then display the values of these variables on the console.

Exercise 2

Write a sequence of Python instructions to declare 1 variable **ch** and initialize it with the value **'hello'**, then modify this same variable to contain the value **'how are you'** . The program should display the content of the variable on the console after modification.

Exercise 3

Write a sequence of Python instructions to declare **2 variables x** and **y**, assigning them the values **3** and **8.5** respectively, then convert the type of these variables to **strings**.
The program should display the **type** of these variables after conversion at the end.

Exercise 4

Write a program that asks the user for their **weight** in **kilograms**, then stores it in a variable. The program should **display the weight** entered by the user at the end.

Exercise 5

Write a sequence of Python instructions to declare a variable **var** and assign it the value **"Hello"** , then the program should check whether the variable **var** is an **integer** or a **string**.
If it's an integer, the program should display **"Integer"** on the console. If it's a string, the program will display **"String"**.

Exercise 6

Write a program that declares the variable **d** and assigns it the value **5**, then checks whether this variable is **greater** or **less** than 0. If the variable is **greater than 0**, the program should display **'Positive'**, otherwise, it should display **'Negative'** .

Exercise 7

Write a program that asks the user for their **age**, then stores it in a variable. The program should check whether the user is **older** or **younger** than **18 years**. If the user's age is **greater than** or **equal** to **18**, the program should display **"The user is of legal age"** , otherwise **"The user is a minor"**.

Exercise 8 : Generating Numbers Using Loops

Write a Python program that displays the numbers from **1 to 20 inclusive** on the console.

Note: You need to create two versions, one with the *for* loop and the other with the *while* loop.

Exercise 9 : Odd Numbers Included in an Interval

Write a Python program that displays only the **odd** numbers between **10** and **20 inclusive**.

Note: You need to create two versions, one with the *for* loop and the other with the *while* loop.

Exercise 10 : List Comprehension

Write the instruction that creates a **list of numbers** from **1** to **10** using **list comprehension**

Exercise 11 : Even Numbers

Write the instruction that creates a list of **even numbers** from **1 to 10** using **list comprehension**.

Exercise 12 : Sort a List

Write the instructions that create the **list L** and **assign it** the value **[6, 8, 3, 4, 1, 12, 2, 9.2]**, then sort the numbers in the list in **ascending order**.
The program should **display the list L** after sorting the numbers.

Exercise 13 : Number of Occurrences of an Element

Write the instructions that create the list L and assign it the value **[3, 2, 2, 1, 9, 1, 2, 3, 7]**, then calculate the **number of occurrences** of the **number 1** in the list L.

xercise 14 : Adding Elements to a List

rite the instructions that create an **empty list L** and then add the tegers **10, 25, 30, 45, 90**, and the strings **"ab"** , **"cd"** , **"ef"** to it.

xercise 15 : List Comprehension

rite a program that creates the **list L** and assigns it the value 2,3,4,5,6,7,8,9,10], then creates a **new list L1** that takes **every third ement** from the list L.
this case, we should end up with the following list: **[1,4,7,10]**.

xercise 16 : Sorting a String

rite the instructions to sort a string in **ascending alphabetical order**.
or testing, let's take the string **c = "france"** .
e program should output **"acefnr"**

xercise 17 : Common Elements Between Two Lists

rite a program that, given two lists **L1** and **L2**, returns a list **L3** ntaining the **common elements** between **L1** and **L2.**

or testing, we will take the lists:
= [9, 8, 7, 14, 3, 2, "a", "p", "hello" , "b"]
 = ["b", 1, 9.2, 6, 3, 9, "p"]

Exercise 18 : Sorting a List of Tuples

Write a program that sorts a **list of tuples**, L, in **ascending order** based on the **second element** of each tuple.
The list we will consider in this exercise is:
L = [("Apple" , 15), ("Banana" , 8), ("Strawberry", 12), ("Kiwi" , 9"Peach", 2)]

The resulting list L **after sorting** should be:
L = [("Peach" ,2), ("Banana" ,8), ("Kiwi" ,9), ("Strawberry" ,12), ("Apple" ,15)]

Exercise 19 : Reverse a String

Write a program that allows you to **reverse a string**.
The program should reverse the variable **ch** containing the phrase **"Hell everyone"**

Exercise 20 : The Values of a Dictionary

Write a program that displays on the console the values of the keys **"Apple"** and **"Banana"** from the dictionary
{"Apple" : 3, "Banana": 7, "Kiwi": 1}

Exercise 21 : Sum of the Values of a Dictionary

Write a program that calculates the **sum** of the **values** in the following dictionary:
{"Apple" : 15, "Banana" : 8, "Strawberry" : 12, "Kiwi" : 9, "Peach" : 2}

Exercise 22 : Using the format() Method

Write a program that truncates a decimal number to 2 digits after the decimal point.
For example, if we take the decimal number **187.632587**, the program should display **187.63**.

Exercise 23 : Using the format() Method

Write a program that formats the string "My name is *myName* and I am *age* years old. I am learning the language *languageName*"
The program should format this string by assigning the content of the following variables:

myName = "Julien" , **age** = 32, **languageName** = "Python"

The program will display on the console: **"My name is Julien and I am 32 years old. I am learning the language Python."**

Exercise 24

Write a program that displays the multiplication table of the **number 8**.
The program should produce the following output:

```
8 x 0 = 0
8 x 1 = 8
8 x 2 = 16
8 x 3 = 24
8 x 4 = 32
8 x 5 = 40
8 x 6 = 48
8 x 7 = 56
8 x 8 = 64
8 x 9 = 72
8 x 10 = 80
```

Exercise 25

Write a program that displays the **directory** where the current Python script is located.

Exercise 26

Write a program that allows you to remove an element from a list. Let's consider the list L = [1, 2, 3, 4, 5] and we want to remove the number 1.

Exercise 27

Write a program that allows you to retrieve the extension of a file.

Exercise 28

Write a program that calculates the **execution time of a script**. Let's take the script from **exercise 24** as an example and calculate its execution time.
The program should **display the multiplication table** from exercise 24 and the **execution time** at the end.

Exercise 29

Write a program that **randomly shuffles** the elements of a list L. For example, let's consider the list **L = [3, 6, 8, 7, 2, 's', 'ch', 'd']**.

Exercise 30 : Generate a Number Randomly

Write a program that randomly returns a number between **20** and **30**.

Exercise 31 : Displaying Patterns

Write a program that displays the following numbers on the console:

```
5 6 7 8 9 10 11 12 13 14 15 16 17 18 19 20
5 6 7 8 9 10 11 12 13 14 15 16 17 18 19 20
5 6 7 8 9 10 11 12 13 14 15 16 17 18 19 20
5 6 7 8 9 10 11 12 13 14 15 16 17 18 19 20
5 6 7 8 9 10 11 12 13 14 15 16 17 18 19 20
5 6 7 8 9 10 11 12 13 14 15 16 17 18 19 20
5 6 7 8 9 10 11 12 13 14 15 16 17 18 19 20
5 6 7 8 9 10 11 12 13 14 15 16 17 18 19 20
```

Exercise 32

Write a program that creates the **variable L** and assigns it the list
[3, 6, 9, 12, 15, 18, 21, 24], then creates a new **list L1** using
list comprehension that contains the numbers from **L divided by 3**.
The program should **display** the **list L1** on the console.

Exercise 33

Write a program that creates the **variable L** and assigns it the list
[-6,5,-3,-1,2,8,-3.6], then creates a **new list L1** using list comprehension
that contains the numbers from **L** that are strictly greater than 0.
The program should **display** the list **L1** at the end.

ercise 34 : Mathematical function

rite a function named **f(a,b,x)** that takes three integers **a,b** and **x** as rameters and returns the result of the following function:

$$f(a,b,x) = a*(x**3) + 2*a*(x**2) + b$$

rification tests:
> f(3,0,1)

> f(0,2,2)

ercise 35 : Presence of an element in a list

rite a function named **CheckPresence(a,L)** that takes a list **L** and an ement **a** as parameters. The function returns **True** if the element **a** ists in the list **L**, and **False** if the element **a** does not exist in the list **L**.

rification tests:
> CheckPresence(2,[1,2,3,4,5,6]
ue

> CheckPresence(-1, [3,6,9,7, "abcr"])
lse

Exercise 36 : Calculation of the sum of digits

Write a program that calculates the **sum of the digits of a number.** The program should **display the result** on the console.

Some examples:
- For the number 149, the program displays 14.
- For the number 3018, the program displays 12.

Exercise 37 : Sum of a list

Write a function called **calculateSum(L)** that takes a list of integers **L** as a parameter and returns the **sum of the values** in this list.

Verification tests:
>> *calculateSum([3,2,6,9,-1,5])*
24

>> *calculateSum([-3,-6,0,1,2,7])*
1

Exercise 38 : Removing Duplicates

Write a function **removeDuplicates(L)** that takes a list of integers **L** as a parameter and returns the list **L** without any duplicate elements in **ascending** order.

Verification tests:
>> *removeDuplicates([0,3,5,7,3,5,1,-1])*
[-1,0,1,3,5,7]

>> *removeDuplicates([0,5,9,10,3.2,1,-3])*
[-3,0,1,3.2,5,9,10]

Exercise 39 : Adding elements to a dictionary

Write a function named **addElementDict(key,value,d)** that takes three parameters as input: a **dictionary d**, a **key** and its associated **value**. The function should **add** this key and value to the dictionary **d**. Finally, the function should return the modified **dictionary d** with the new key-value pair.

Verification tests:
>> addElementDict("baptiste" , 29, {"julien" : 14, "laurent" : 31})
{"julien" : 14, "laurent" : 31, "baptiste" : 29}

>> addElementDict("weight" , 65.3, {})
{"weight" : 65.3}

Exercise 40 : Recreation of the max function

Write a function **maximum(L)** that takes a list of integers as a parameter and returns the **largest value.**

Note: The idea is not to use the already available **max()** function in Python.

Verification tests:
>> maximum([-9,2,4,1,8])
8

>> maximum([-3,1,7,6,2,3])
7

Exercise 41 : Sum of a Sublist

Write the code for the function **sumSubList(L,i,j)** which takes three parameters a list **L**, a starting calculation index **i,** and an ending calculation index **j**. The function should return the **sum of the numbers** located between **indices i** and in the list.

Verification tests:
>> sumSubList([4,10,12,16,18], 2, 4)
46

>> sumSubList([2,4,6,8,10,12], 0, 2)
12

Exercise 42 : Pattern Creation

Write a program that displays the star pyramid below:

```
        *
        **
        ****
        ******
        ********
        **********
```

Exercise 43 : Recreation of the min function

Write a function **minimum(L)** which takes a list of integers **L** as a parameter and returns the **smallest value**.

Verification tests:
>> *minimum([-9,2,4,1,8])*
-9

>> *minimum([-3,1,7,6,2,3])*
-3

Exercise 44 : Recreation of the len function

Write a function **length(L)** which takes a **list of integers L** as a parameter and returns the **number of elements** in this list.

Verification tests:
>> *length([3,6,7, "abde" , [1,3,57], True])*
6

>> *length([ ])*
0

Exercise 45 : Calculating the average of a list numbers

Write a function **averageList(L)** which takes a list of integers as a parameter and returns the average of a list L.

Verification tests:
>> averageList([1,2,3,4,5,6,7])
4.0

>> averageList([3,0,-1,5,6,9,17])
5.571428571428571

Exercise 46 : Divisors of an integer

Write a function **divisor(n)** which takes an **integer n** as a parameter and returns a list containing all the **positive divisors** of **n** in **ascending** order.

Verification tests:
>> divisor(3)
[1,3]

>> divisor(9)
[1,3,9]

xercise 47 : Capitalization Check

rite a function **checkCapitals(sentence)** which takes a *sentence* as a ⸱rameter and checks if the sentence contains at **least one uppercase** ⸱tter. If that's the case, the function should return **True**; otherwise, it ⸱ould return **False**

⸱rification tests:
> *checkCapitals("Vegetables are good for health")*
ue

> *checkCapitals("this is the best book in python")*
⸱lse

xercise 48 : List Concatenation

⸱rite a function **concatList(L1,L2,L3)** which takes three lists **L1**, **L2** et **L3** ⸱s parameters and returns the **concatenation** of these three lists.

⸱rification tests:
> *concatList([0,9,8],[2,6,9],[True,False, "abc"])*
⸱,9,8,2,6,9,True,False, "abc"]

> *concatList([[38,-1],3,-9], ["xz", "France"], [ ])*
⸱38,-1],3,-9, "xz" , "France"]

Exercise 49 : Calculating the Number of Values in a Dictionary

Write a function **valueCountDict(d)** which takes a **dictionary d** as a parameter and returns the **number of values** contained in the lists associated with the keys.

Note: for the purpose of this exercise, it is assumed that all values associated with keys are in the form of lists.

Verification tests:
>> *valueCountDict({"a" : [1,2,3], "b" : [3, "p"], "c" : [8]})*
6

>> *valueCountDict({"Julie" : [12, 60.1] , "Fred" : [26, 75.6], "David" : [ ]})*
4

Exercise 50 : Concatenation of dictionaries

Write a function **concatDict(d1,d2)** which takes two dictionaries **d1** and **d2** as parameters and returns the **concatenation** of these two dictionaries **d1** and **d2**.

Verification tests:
>> *concatDict({"a" : 3, "b" : 6},{"c" : 2, "d" : -1})*
{"a" : 3, "b" : 6, "c" : 2, "d" : -1}

>> *concatDict({"d" : [2.9,4.1]}, {"p" : [ ]})*
{"d" : [2.9,4.1], "p" : [ ]}

Exercise 51 : Calculating the factorial of a number

Write a function **computeFactorial(n)** that calculates **the factorial of a number** *(in the mathematical sense)* and returns the **result** obtained after this calculation.

Verification tests:
>> *computeFactorial(3)*
6

>> *computeFactorial(9)*
362880

>> *computeFactorial(0)*
1

Exercise 52 : Divisors & Multiples

Write a function **divisorsMult(n,a,threshold)** that finds the numbers *(from 0 up to a given threshold)* divisible by **n** and not multiples of **a**.

Verification tests:
>> *divisorsMult(5,2,100)*
[5,15,25,35,45,55,65,75,85,95]

>> *divisorsMult(11,3,85)*
[11,22,44,55,77]

Exercise 53 : Presence of a Vowel in a String

Write a function **hasVowel(sentence)** which takes a sentence as a parameter and checks if a sentence **contains a vowel or not**. If the sentence contains a vowel, the function returns **True**; otherwise, it returns **False**.

Note: we will assume that the vowels in English are as follows: *(a,e,i,o,u,y)*

Verification tests:
>> *hasVowel("I'm going to take my shower")*
True

>> *hasVowel("rbhpm")*
False

Exercise 54 : Removing Spaces in a Sentence

Write a function **removeSpaces(sentence)** which takes a **sentence** as a string parameter and returns the **same sentence** without spaces *(if they exist)* between words.

Verification tests:
>> *removeSpaces("France is beautiful!")*
Franceisbeautiful

>> *removeSpaces("I will take my bike.")*
Iwilltakemybike

20

Exercise 55 : Position of an Element in a List

Write a function **EltPositionList(L,x)** which takes a list of **elements L** and an **element x** as parameters, then **returns the index** *(or indices)* where the **element x** is located in the **list L**. The function should return a list of indices. If the element **x is not in the list L**, then the program will display on the console: **"Element x is not in list L"** .

Verification tests:
>> *EltPositionList([1,2,3,6,8,7,3],3)*
[2,6]

>> *EltPositionList([6,8,9,1,3,7],-1)*
Element -1 is not in list [6,8,9,1,3,7]

Exercise 56 : Filter words by length

Write a function **filterWords(sentence,minLength)** which takes a **sentence** as a parameter and **filters out words** with a length **strictly less** than the parameter **minLength**. The function should return the same sentence **without the filtered words**.

Note: It is assumed that words in a sentence are separated by spaces.

Verification tests:
>> *filterWords("Hello how are you?", 4)*
Hello you?

>> *filterWords("Where do you come from?", 5)*
Where from?

Exercise 57 : Reverse the Order of Words

Write a function **reverseSentence(sentence)** which takes a **sentence** as a parameter and reverses the order of words in the sentence. The function should return the **sentence with the words reversed**.

Note: It is assumed that words in a sentence are separated by spaces.

Verification tests:
>> *reverseSentence("could you get me a coffee?")*
coffee? a me get you could

>> *reverseSentence("Apple")*
Apple

Exercise 58 : Number of Occurrences in a List

Write a function **occurrenceCount(L)** which takes **a list L** as a parameter and returns **a list of tuples**, where each tuple corresponds to an element from **list L** along with its **number of occurrences** in the list.

Verification tests:
>> *occurrenceCount([-4,8,-3,2,1,2,7,9,-3,8,1])*
[(-4,1),(8,2),(-3,2),(2,2),(1,2),(7,1),(9,1)]

>> *occurrenceCount(["a" , 3, 4, "b", "a", 3])*
[("a" ,2),(3,2),(4,1),("b" ,1)]

xercise 59 : Union of lists without duplication

rite a function **unionList(L1,L2,L3)** which takes **three lists** of integers
, **L2**, and **L3** as parameters, and returns a list in **ascending order** that
presents the **union of these three lists** without **any duplicate**
imbers.

erification tests:
> *unionList([3,6,9,3],[1,0,3],[12,6,0])*
1,3,6,9,12]

> *unionList([7,44,-3],[ ], [7,2,7])*
3,2,7,44]

xercise 60 : Calculation of the GCD

rite a function **calculateGCD(a,b)** which takes **two integers a** and **b** as
rameters and calculates the **greatest common divisor** *(GCD)* using the
clidean algorithm.

minder: The Euclidean division of **a** by **b** is written as follows: $a = b*q + r$,
here **q** is the **quotient** and **r** is the **remainder** of the **division**.

erification tests:
> *calculateGCD(3,5)*

> *calculateGCD(5,15)*

Exercise 61 : Reading a file

Write a function **readFile(filePath)** which takes the full path of the file *filePath* as a parameter and **returns its content**. The content of the file should be **displayed** on the console.

Note: for this exercise, you should create a text file with content to test your function.

Verification tests:
>> readFile("C:test.txt")
*****File content****

Exercise 62 : Number of Occurrences of a Word in a File

Write a function **countOccFile(filePath,word)** which takes the file path *filePath* and a *word* as parameters. The function should return the number of occurrences of the *word* in the file provided as a parameter.

Note: we assume that words are separated by spaces.

Verification tests:
>> countOccFile("test.txt", "the")
*****Number of occurrences of "the" in your file****

Exercise 63 : Delete a Character from a File

Write a function **removeChar(filePath,character)** which takes the file path **filePath** and a **character** as parameters. The function should **remove** the **character** provided as a parameter from the specified file.

Verification tests:
>> *removeChar("test.txt", ",")*
*****File content without " , " ****

Exercise 64 : Presence of a number in a file

Write a function **presenceNumber(filePath)** which takes the file path *filePath* as a parameter and checks if the file **contains a number**. The function returns **True** if the file contains a **number** and **False** otherwise.

Verification tests:
>> *presenceNumber("test.txt")*
*****True ou False*****

Exercise 65 : Number of files in a folder

Write a function **fileCount(folderPath)** which takes the folder path *folderPath* as a parameter and returns the **number of files** contained in the specified folder.

Verification tests:
>> fileCount("test")
*****Number of files in test folder*****

Exercise 66 : Write in a file

Write a function **writeFile(fileName, text)** which takes the file name *fileName* and the *text* that you want to write to the file as parameters.
The function will allow us to have a file containing the *text* provided as a parameter.

Note: we assume in this exercise that the text file is initially empty

Verification tests:
>> writeFile("test.txt", "Hello, my name is Gregory and I am 30 years old")
*****The file should contain the text provided as a parameter*****

Exercise 67 : The key with the maximum number of unique values

Write a function **maxKeyUniqueValuesDict(d)** which takes a **dictionary d** as a parameter and **returns the key with the highest number of unique values**.

Note: in this exercise, we assume that the values of all keys are in the form of lists

Verification tests:

>> *maxKeyUniqueValuesDict({"a" : [9,10,9,7,3,1], "b" : [5,3,2,2,2], "c" : [1,1,1,1,1,8,2]})*

a

>> *maxKeyUniqueValuesDict({"dtg" : [6,8,1], "fgb" : [2.5, "a"], "klm" : ["p" ,3,3]})*

dtg

Exercise 68 : Ask the user for a list

Write a program that prompts the user to **enter a list of integers** from the console. The program should store this list in a variable **user_list** and display it at the end of the program.

Note: The function we have at our disposal to interact with the user is **input()**, which returns a **string as output**. The goal of the exercise is to use this function to obtain a list of elements by the end of the program.

Exercise 69 : Number of days and hours

Write a function **daysHoursCount(startDate,endDate)** which takes two input parameters: the start date *startDate* and the end date *endDate*. This function will allow us to calculate the **number of days** and the **number of hours** between the **start** and **end dates** provided as parameters. The function should return the tuple **(DayCount, HourCount)**

Verification tests:
>> *daysHoursCount("2022/05/15", "2022/06/20")*
(36, 864)

>> *daysHoursCount("2022/04/1", "2022/04/27")*
(26, 624)

Exercise 70 : Generate a Password Randomly

Write a function **generatePassword(characters, passwordLength)** which takes a **list of characters** *characters* and the **length of the password** *passwordLength* as parameters, then **randomly generates a password** with the specified **length** and **characters**. The function should return the password as a string.

Exercise 71 : Trigonometric function

Write a function **trigoFunct(x)** that takes a parameter **x** and returns the result of the function **f(x) = cos(x)*sin(x) + sin(x) + 8**.

Note: In this exercise, we will be using the **math** module.

Verification tests:
>> *trigoFunct(math.pi/4)*
9.207106781186548

>> *trigoFunct(math.pi)*
8

28

xercise 72

rite a program that stores in a list **L** all **positive integers** with three digits in
e form **abc**, such that for each integer, the **sum** of its digits **a+b+c** is a divisor
the product of its digits **a*b*c**.
ne program should display the list containing these integers at the end.

or example: the number 514 satisfies this property, as **5+1+4 = 10** is a divisor
5*1*4 = 20

Exercise 73

this exercise, we will revisit the solution from **exercise 37**, which involves
riting a function *calculateSum(L)*.
ne goal of the exercise is to recreate the same function, but this time using a
cursive approach.

Exercise 74

/rite a recursive function **fibonacciSequence(N)** that takes a **positive natural**
umber **N positif** as a parameter and returns the **element** at index **N** of the
ibonacci sequence.

eminder: we are interested in the sequence of integers defined by **F1 = 1**,
2 = 1 and for any natural number N, **F(N+2) = F(N+1) + F(N)**

erification tests:
> *fibonacciSequence(25)*
5025

> *fibonacciSequence(45)*
134903170

Exercise 75 : Mutual recursive functions

A number **n** is **even** if **n-1** is **odd**, and vice versa, if a number **n** is **odd**, then **n-** is **even**.
Write two **mutually recursive** functions **isEven(n)** et **isOdd(n)** to determine whether a **number n** is **even** or **odd**.

Verification tests:
>> *isEven(5)*
False

>> *isOdd(7)*
True

Exercise 76 : Recreating the join method

Write a function **join(L, character)** hat transforms a list *L* into a string using t separator *character* passed as a parameter.

Verification tests:
>> *join(["Hello", "Aurélie"], " ")*
"Hello Aurélie"

>> *join(["Hi", " How are you?"], " , ")*
"Hi, How are you?"

Exercise 77 : Recreating the replace method

Write a function **replaceString(sentence,oldWord,newWord)** that allows replacing the word *oldWord* with the word *newWord* in the string parameter *sentence*.
The function should return the **sentence** with the *newWord* replacing the *oldWord*.

Verification tests:
>> *replaceString("Hello Aurélie", "Aurélie", "Mathilde")*
"Hello Mathilde"

>> *replaceString("I'm 50 years old", "50", "35")*
"I'm 35 years old"

Exercise 78 : Recreating the split method

Write a function **split(sentence, character)** that transforms a *sentence* into a **list** using the separator *character.*

Verification tests:
>> *split("Hello Aurélie", " ")*
["Hello", "Aurélie"]

>> *split("Hi, how are you?", " , ")*
["Hi", " how are you?"]

Exercise 79 : Recreating the isdigit() method

Write a function **isdigit(string)** that checks whether the *string* is a **number** or **not**. The function returns **True** if the string is a number and **False** otherwise.

Verification tests:
>> *isdigit("125920")*
True

>> *isdigit("edgte9be")*
False

Exercise 80 : Palindrome numbers

Write a function **isPalindrome(nbr)** that takes a positive integer *nbr* as a parameter and returns **True** if *nbr* is a **palindrome**, and **False** if it is not.

Reminder: a palindrome number is a natural number **greater than 10** that reads the same **forwards** as it does **backwards**.

For example, the numbers 69596, 4231324, 212 are palindrome numbers.

Verification tests:
>> *isPalindrome(10)*
False

>> *isPalindrome(919)*
True

Exercise 81 : Palindrome numbers

The largest palindrome number obtained as the product of two two-digit integers is **9009 = 91 x 99**.
Write a program that finds the largest palindrome number obtained as the product of two **three-digit integers**.

Note: You can use the **isPalindrome** function from the previous exercise.

Exercise 82 : Circular prime numbers

Write a function **isCircularPrime(nbr)** that takes a positive integer *nbr* as a parameter and tests whether a number is a **circular prime**. The function returns **True** if the number passed as a parameter **is a circular prime** and **False** otherwise.

Reminder: A number is considered a **circular prime** if its **digit rotations** are **prime numbers**. For example, the number **197** is a **circular prime** because **197, 971, and 719 are prime numbers** *(the first digit of 197 is moved to the end to get 971, then the 9 is moved to the end of 971 to get 719).*
Other examples of circular prime numbers include 19391, 19937, 71, 37, 31, 9377, etc.

Hint: It is advisable to implement a function **isPrime(nbr)** that checks if a number is prime, and then use it in **isCircularPrime(nbr)**

Verification tests:
>> *isCircularPrime(9377)*
True

>> *isCircularPrime(36)*
False

Exercise 83 : Number with distinct digits

Write a function **isDistinct(number)** that takes a **positive integer** as a parameter and **checks if all the digits** in this *number* are **distinct**. The function should return **True** if the *number* contains only distinct digits and **False** otherwise.

Verification tests:
>> isDistinct(9647)
True

>> isDistinct(1343)
False

Exercise 84

Write a function **codeSum(number)** that takes a positive integer *number* **greater than 100** as a parameter and allows determining a code from this number, following the steps below:

> - **Step 1:** Sum the digits of the *number* passed as a parameter.
> - **Step 2:** Repeat the calculation of the obtained sum *(in Step 1)* until it falls between 1 and 9.

The code will be the original *number* with the last obtained **sum added to its left**.

Verification tests:
>> codeSum(69810)
669810

>> codeSum(3201)
63201

Exercise 85 : Dichotomic search

Write a function **dichotomicSearch(L,elt)** qthat takes as parameters a list *L* sorted in **ascending order** and an element *elt*. The function should allow us to find the element *elt* in the list *L* using **dichotomic search**. If the element is found, the function returns **True**; otherwise, it returns **False**.

Verification tests:
> *dichotomicSearch([6,9,15,36,41,43,47], 41)*
True

> *dichotomicSearch([-9,-1,3,4,7,11], 0)*
False

Reminder of the dichotomic search algorithm:

Context: In a sorted **list L of values**, we are trying to determine if a value **elt** is present in the list **L**.

Dichotomy search steps:
- We examine the element in the **middle of the list L** and compare it to **elt**.
- If they are **equal**, the algorithm stops, and the element is found; otherwise, we continue the search in the **first** or **second half** of the array.
- If, in the end, we have reduced the portion of the list to the point that it **no longer contains any elements, the search stops with a failure: elt** is not in **L**.

Exercise 86 : Pythagorean triplet x,y,z

A Pythagorean triplet is a triplet (x, y, z) of integers such that x < y < z and x**2+y**2 = z**2. There is a unique Pythagorean triplet such that: x+y+z = 1000. Que vaut x*y*z?

*Note: ** denotes exponentiation, and * denotes multiplication*

Exercise 87 : File processing

Write a function **processFile(filePath)** that takes a text file as a parameter and creates another text file *(using a path of your choice)* that will contain the same content as the file passed as a parameter but without line breaks.

>> processFile("test.txt")
******A file without line breaks******

Exercise 88 : Bubble sort

Write a function **ascendingSort(L)** that takes a list of integers **L** as a parameter and sorts the list in **ascending order.** The function should return the **list L** with integers sorted from the **smallest** to the **largest**.

Verification tests:
>> ascendingSort([6,1,9,-6,1,8,7])
[-6,1,1,6,7,8,9]

>> ascendingSort([-3,5.3,2,7,1,2.3,9,5])
[-3,1,2,2.3,5.3,7,9.5]

Exercise 89 : Creating a class Person

Write a Python class named **Person** that possesses three attributes defining certain characteristics of a real person: **height (in m)**, **weight (in kg)** and **age**.

This Python class will have two methods:
- **calculateBMI(self)** which calculates the BMI of the person.
- **interpretBMI(self)** which displays:
    * *"The BMI calculation indicates that the person is underweight (thinness)"* if the result returned by **calculateBMI(self)** is **less than** or **equal** to **18.5**.
    * *"The person is obese"* if the result is **greater** than or **equal** to **30**.
    * Otherwise, it displays *"The person is overweight or has a normal body weight"*

Reminder: The Body Mass Index *(BMI)* is calculated using the formula *weight/(height**2)*.

Verification tests:
>> *julien = Person(1.87, 95, 26)*
>> *julien.calculateBMI(self)*
27.16
>> *julien.interpretBMI(self)*
"The person is overweight or has a normal body weight"

Exercise 90 : Rectangle class

Write a class **Rectangle** that has two attributes: **width (in cm)** and **length (in cm)**.

The **Rectangle** class should contain the following methods:
- **Perimeter(self)** which calculates the perimeter of the rectangle.
- **Area(self)** which calculates the area of the rectangle.

Verification tests:
>> rectangle1 = Rectangle(10,15)
>> rectange1.width
10
>> rectange1.length
15
>> rectangle1.Perimeter()
50
>> rectangle1.Area()
150

Exercise 91 : Inheriting a class

Write a class **Parallelepiped** that inherits from the **Rectangle** class from the previous exercise. The **Parallelepiped** class should contain, in addition to the inherited attributes, the attribute **height (in cm).**

The **Parallepiped** class should have the following method:
- **Volume(self)** which calculates the volume of the parallelepiped

>> parallelepiped1 = Parallelepiped(9,5,2)
>> parallelepiped1.Perimeter()
28
>> parallelepiped1.Volume()
90

Exercise 92 : BankAccount class

Write a class **BankAccount** that allows us to manage a bank account. This class will have two attributes: **name** and **balance**.
By default, the attributes have the following values: name = "Maxime", balance = 600.

This class should include the following three methods:
- **deposit(self,amount)** which will **add** a certain *amount* to the balance.
- **withdraw(self,amount)** which will **withdraw** a certain *amount* from the balance.
- **__repr__(self)** which will display the **account holder's name** and the balance of their account.

Verification tests:
>> *account1 = BankAccount("Julie" , 1000)*
>> *account1.deposit(400)*
>> *account1.withdraw(100)*
>> *account1*
The balance of Julie's bank account is 1300 euros.

>> *account2 = BankAccount()*
>> *account2.deposit(500)*
>> *account2*
The balance of Maxime's bank account is 1100 euros.

Exercise 93 : Car class

Write a class **Car** that allows us to manage rental automobiles. The class will have 4 attributes representing various characteristics: **brand, color, driverName** and **startingKm**.
By default, these attributes have the following values:
brand = "peugeot", color = "dark", driverName = "None",
startingKm = 16900

This class should include the following three methods:
- **chooseDriver(self, driverName)** which will designate or change the driver's name for the car.
- **calculateDistance(self, finalKm)** which will calculate the distance traveled by the driver during the rental period.
- **displayInfo(self)** which will display the current state of the car, including the driver's name, **brand, color**, and **current mileage**.

Verification tests:
>> car1 = Car()
>> car1.chooseDriver("Patrick")
>> car1.calculateDistance(20000)
3100
>> car1.displayInfo()
The black Peugeot car driven by Patrick currently has a mileage of 20000 km.

xercise 94 : operator overload

rite a class **Point2D** that represents a point in a 2D space. Our class ould contain two attributes: **x** and **y**.

this exercise, we want to perform some operations with instances eated from the **Point2D** class using standard operators such as **+**, **-**, *****, **c**. To achieve this, we need to create the following special methods for e class:

- **__add__(self,p)** which allows us to perform the operation **p1 + p2**
- **__sub__(self,p)** which allows us to perform the operation **p1 - p2**
- **__mul__(self,p)** which allows us to perform the operation **p1*p2**
- **__truediv__(self,p)** qwhich allows us to perform the operation **p1/p2**

minder: Operator overloading involves creating **special methods** in the ss that allow us to use **standard operators** such as **+, -, *, /**, and so on.

rification tests:
> p1 = Point2D(3,2)
> p2 = Point2D(1,4)
> p1 - p2
-2)
> p1 + p2
6)
> p1/p2
0,0.5)

Exercise 95 : operator overload

Write a class **ComplexNumber** that represents complex numbers *(in th mathematical sense)*. This class will have two attributes: **real** and **img**

Reminder: a **complex number** consists of a **real component** and an **imaginary** component. This number is written in the form **5 + 3i**, where the number **5** represents the **real part** and the **number 3** represents the **imaginary** part.

In this exercise, we want the following results when calling an instance of the class or using *print()* with this instance:

Verification tests:
>> nbr1 = ComplexNumber(2,7)
>> nbr1
2 + 7i
>> print(nbr1)
2 + 7i

To achieve this, we need to create the following special methods:

- __**str**__(**self**) which allows us to have the correct display using **print()**
- __**repr**__(**self**) which allows us to have the correct display when calling a instance.

Exercise 96 : Customized list class

Write a class **CustomList** which is a custom list class. Our custom list should **only contain numbers** and **not strings** or **booleans**. In our custom list, **duplicates are not allowed**.

In this exercise, you need to create methods that allow us to perform the following operations:

Verification tests:
```
>> L1 = CustomList(5,2,3,7,9)
>> print(L1)
[5,2,3,7,9]
>> L1.append(2)
The number 2 already exists in the list [5,2,3,7,9]
>> L1.append("abc")
Forbidden operation: It is not possible to add type < class 'str'> to the list
>> L1.append(10)
>> print(L1)
[5,2,3,7,9,10]
```

Exercise 97 : Customized string class

Write a class **CustomString** which is a custom string class. Our custom string should not contain **numbers**, **commas**, or **periods**.

In this exercise, you need to create methods that allow us to perform the following operations:

>> *string1 = CustomString("He,llo")*
The created instance should only contain alphabetical letters
The character " , " will be removed
>> *string1 + " , "*
You cannot add ',' to the string
>> *string1 + " . "*
You cannot add '.' to the string
>> *string2 = string1 + " How are you? "*
>> *string2*
Hello How are you?

Exercise 98 : Ordering a dictionary by key

Write a function **orderDict(d)** that takes a dictionary **d** as a parameter and returns a dictionary ordered in **ascending order** based on the **keys of the dictionary**.

Guideline: the keys of the dictionary **d** should not be a mix of **strings** and **numbers**.

Verification tests:
>> *orderDict({"c" : 3, "a" : 9, "e" : 1})*
{"a": 9, "c" : 3, "e" : 1}

>> *orderDict({8 : 9, 2 : 3, 9 : 11})*
{2:3,8:9,9:11}

Exercise 99 : The maximum sum of a sub-list

Write a function **largestSum(L)** that takes a list **L** as a parameter and determines the **largest sum** obtained by summing the elements of **all possible subsequences** of the list **L**.
The function should return the **subsequence list** that yields the largest sum as well as the **maximum sum** found.

Reminder: a subsequence is a sequence of numbers in the list L

Verification tests:
> largestSum([-8,-4,6,8,-6,10,-4,-4])
18 , [6,8,-6,10])

> largestSum([-6,1,8,-7,1,9,-1,2])
13 , [1,8,-7,1,9,-1,2])

Exercise 100 : Separate elements 0 and 1

Write a function **separateElements(L)** that takes a list **L** as a parameter where the elements are either **0** or **1**, and **separates the 0s from the 1s** by placing the 0s at the beginning of the list and the 1s afterwards.

Verification tests:
> separateElements([0,1,0,1,1,0,0,1,0,1])
0,0,0,0,0,1,1,1,1,1]

> separateElements([1,0,0,0,1,0,1,1,1,0,1,1,0,0,0,1])
0,0,0,0,0,0,0,0,1,1,1,1,1,1,1,1]

Exercise 1 Correction

```
## Exercise 1

## Variable Declaration
a = 1
b = "France"
c = 36.2

## Console Display
print(a)
print(b)
print(c)
```

Program results

```
1
France
36.2
```

Comments:
- The first three lines are used to declare a variable. By writing **a = 1**, the program stores the **value 1** in the **variable a**.
- The **print()** function will allow us to display the content of the variable on the console.

Exercise 2 Correction

```
## Exercise 2

## Declaration of variable ch
ch = "hello"
## Variable modification
ch = "how are you"
##  Console display
print(ch)
```

how are you

46

Exercise 3 Correction

```
## Exercise 3

## Variable Declaration Storing
## Numeric Values
x = 3
y = 8.5

## Conversion of Numeric
## Variables to Strings
x = str(x)
y = str(y)

## Displaying Variable Types
print(type(x))
print(type(y))

<class 'str'>
<class 'str'>
```

Comments:

In Python, it is entirely possible to convert the type of a variable to another type *(casting)*. In our case, we want to convert a numeric variable to a string variable. For this purpose, we have the **str()** function at our disposal, which allows us to do so. Other types of conversion are possible using the **int()** and **float()** functions.

To know the type of a variable, you can use the **type()** function by specifying the variable or object in parentheses that you want to know the type of.

Exercise 4 Correction

```
## Exercise 4

weight = input("What is your weight in kilograms? ")

print("The user's weight is:", weight)

What is your weight in kilograms? 75.6
The user's weight is: 75.6
```

Comments:

- To interact with the user, Python provides us with the **input()** function, whic takes a **string parameter** *(often used to describe the information requested from the user)* and returns the **information entered by the user as a string.**

Exercise 5 Correction

```
## Exercise 5

var = "Hello"

## Condition:
## If the variable is a string:
if type(var) == str:
    ## then "String" is displayed
    print("String")

## If it's an integer
elif type(var) == int:
    ## then "Integer" is displayed
    print("Integer")
```

```
String
```

Comments:

- In programming, the use of **conditional statements** is very useful when we want to **check a condition** before executing a set of instructions. In this exercise, we have two different displays depending on the type of the variable Therefore, **distinguishing cases** is necessary using conditional statements.

Exercise 6 Correction

```
## Exercise 6

d = 5

## If the variable is positive
if d >= 0 :
    print("Positive")

## If not positive
else:
    print("Negative")
```

```
Positive
```

Comments:

- In this case, we check using the first condition **(d >= 0)** if the variable **d** is **positive**. All other cases **(d < 0)** are covered in the **"else"**

Exercise 7 Correction

```
## Exercise 7

## Request user age
age = input("How old are you? ")

## convert age to int
age = int(age)

## Case distinction
if age >= 18:
    print("The user is of legal age")
else:
    print("The user is a minor")
```

```
How old are you? 18
The user is of legal age
```

49

Comments:

- The **input()** function returns the **age** entered by the user as a string. Therefore, in order to compare the user's age to 18 *(in the conditional statement)*, it would be necessary to convert the **age** variable to an **integer** value.

Exercise 8 Correction

```
## Exercise 8

## 1st version with for loop
for i in range(1,21):
    print(i)

## 2nd version with while loop
counter = 1
while counter <= 20:
    print(counter)
    counter += 1
```

Comments:

- In programming, we often need to execute an instruction **multiple times** to accomplish a given task. **Loops** allow us to do this

- There are two types of loops in Python: the *for* loop and the *while* loop. The *for* loop allows us to execute a set of instructions a **well-defined number of times**, while the *while* loop allows us to execute a set of instructions **as long as a condition is met**.

- The **range(start,stop[,step])** function provides us with a sequence of integer numbers between the *start* and *stop-1* parameters. This function is often used with the *for* loop, as it allows us to define the list of integers we want to iterate through. Additionally, you can add the optional *step* parameter to specify the step size. By default, the *step* is 1.
In our case, the function **range(1, 21)** returns a **list of integers** from **1 to 20**.

Exercise 9 Correction

```
## Exercise 9

## 1st version with for loop
for i in range(10,21):
    if i%2 == 1:
        print(i)

## 2nd version with while loop
counter = 10
while counter <= 20:
    if counter%2 == 1:
        print(counter)
    counter += 1
```

```
11
13
15
17
19
```

Comments:

- In Python, there are several operators, including:
"+" : for addition *(a + b)*
"-" : for subtraction *(a - b)*
"/" : for division *(a / b)*
"%" : for remainder of division *(a % b)*
"//" : for integer division *(a//b)*
"*" : for multiplication *(a*b)*

- In this exercise, to determine if a number is odd, you would need to check if the **remainder of dividing** the number by **2** is equal to **1**.
(equivalent to number%2 = 1)

Exercise 10 Correction

```
## Exercise 10


L = [i for i in range(1,11)]
print(L)
```

```
[1, 2, 3, 4, 5, 6, 7, 8, 9, 10]
```

Comments:

- List comprehensions allow you to **generate a list** in a **single expression** instead of using multiple statements. The advantage of using a list comprehension is to make the code more readable and save time by avoiding writing multiple lines of code.

Exercise 11 Correction

```
## Exercise 11

## Comprehension list containing only pairs numbers
L = [i for i in range(1,11) if i%2 == 0]
print(L)
```

```
[2, 4, 6, 8, 10]
```

Exercise 12 Correction

```
## Exercise 12

## Declaration of the list L
L = [6,8,3,4,1,12,2,9.2]
## sort list L in ascending order
L.sort()
## Displaying the list L
print(L)
```

```
[1, 2, 3, 4, 6, 8, 9.2, 12]
```

Comments:

To sort a list in **ascending** order, Python provides the *sort()* method, which arranges the elements from **smallest to largest** *(if the list contains numeric values)*, or in **alphabetical order from A to Z** *(if the list contains letter strings)*.

To sort in **descending** order, simply change the *reverse* parameter *(which is false by default)* to **True**. This results in:
> *L. sort(reverse = True)*

Exercise 13 Correction

```
## Exercise 13

## Declaration of the list L
L = [3,2,2,1,9,1,2,3,7]
## Number of occurrences
L.count(1)
```

2

Comments:

- The method *count(element)* returns the number of occurrences of an element in a list. If the element does not exist in the given list, the *count()* method returns 0.

Exercise 14 Correction

```
## Exercise 14

## 1st Method
## Empty list
L = []
## adding elements
L += [10,25,30,45,90,"ab","cd","ef"]
print(L)

## 2nd method
L = []
elt_to_add = [10,25,30,45,90,"ab","cd","ef"]

for elt in elt_to_add:
    ## add element 'elt'
    L.append(elt)
print(L)
```

```
[10, 25, 30, 45, 90, 'ab', 'cd', 'ef']
```

Comments:

- There are several methods to add elements to a list:

1) The first one uses the list concatenation operator **"+"**: adding two lists together results in a new list **containing the elements of both lists**.

2) The second method uses the *append(element)* method: this allows us to add an element to the **end of a list**. To add multiple elements using this method, you can use a *for* loop to repeat the instruction as many times as needed.

Exercise 15 Correction

```
## Exercise 15

## Declaration of the list L
L = [1,2,3,4,5,6,7,8,9,10]
## Declaration of the empty list L1
L1 = []
## iterating through all elements of L
for i in range(len(L)):
    ## keeping only 1 element out of 3
    if i%3 == 0:
        L1.append(L[i])

print(L1)
```

```
[1, 4, 7, 10]
```

Comments:

- It is entirely possible to obtain list **L1 using list comprehensions**. However, we have chosen to provide you with another solution *(without list comprehensions)* in order to be familiar with as many techniques as possible.

Exercise 16 Correction

```
## Exercise 16

## string declaration
c = "france"
## order the string in ascending order
c = sorted(c)
## convert the resulting list into a string
c = "".join(c)
print(c)
```

```
acefnr
```

Comments:

- The *sorted(string)* function allows you to obtain a list consisting of each element of the string passed as a parameter, **sorted in ascending order** *(by default, following alphabetical order from A to Z)*. For example, **sorted('belgium')** gives us: **['b', 'e', 'g', 'i', 'l', 'm', 'u']**.

- It is possible to sort in **descending order** *(from Z to A)* by passing the parameter **reverse = True** in the function: **sorted(string, reverse=True)**.

Exercise 17 Correction

```
## Exercise 17

## Declaration of the lists we will use
L1 = [9,8,7,14,3,2,"a","p","hello","b"]
L2 = ["b",1,9.2,6,3,9,"p"]

## conversion of the lists to sets
## then take the intersection of these two sets
L3 = set(L2).intersection(set(L1))
## convert the set L3 to a list
L3 = list(L3)
print(L3)

[9, 3, 'p', 'b']
```

Comments:

- In this exercise, we introduced a new concept: **sets.**
Sets are an unordered collection of elements *(no specific order)* without indexes *(you cannot select an element by its index)*, and **they cannot have duplicate elements**.

- The *Intersection()* method allows you to obtain the **common elements** between two sets. There are other methods for sets, such as *union()*, *symmetric_difference()*, etc.

Exercise 18 Correction

```
## Exercise 18

## creation of a list of tuples
L = [("Apple",15), ("Banana" ,8), ("Strawberry",12), ("Kiwi",9), ("Peach",2)]
## sort the list of tuples in ascending order
## according to the second element of the tuples
L.sort(key = lambda x : x[1])
print(L)

[('Peach', 2), ('Banana', 8), ('Kiwi', 9), ('Strawberry', 12), ('Apple', 15)]
```

Comments:

- When dealing with a list of tuples, it's important to determine **the position of the element** *(or multiple elements)* within the tuple by which we want to sort our list. In our case, we wanted to **sort based on the 2nd element** of the tuple *(which is the quantity of the fruit)*

- The element by which we want to sort our list of tuples is indicated in the **"key"** parameter of the *sort()* method.

Exercise 19 Correction

```
## Exercise 19

ch = "Hello everyone"
## reverse the string ch
ch_reverse = ch[::-1]
print(ch_reverse)

enoyreve olleH
```

Comments:

- The instruction **ch[::-1]** refers to the syntax *ch[start:end:step]*, with:
start : the starting index for selecting the string ch
end : the ending index for selecting the string ch
pas : the step for selecting elements from the **string ch**. If the **step is 2**, for example, every second element of the **string ch** will be selected.

- By specifying a **step of -1** without **start** and **end** indexes, the string is reversed.

Exercise 20 Correction

```
## Exercise 20

## declaration of the dictionary d
d = {"Apple":3, "Banana":7, "Kiwi" : 1}
## select the value of the key 'Apple'
print(d["Apple"])
## select the value of the key 'Banana'
print(d["Banana"])
```

```
3
7
```

Comments:

- In Python, a dictionary allows you to gather elements that are identified by a key.
Each key in a dictionary is associated with a value. In our example, the key **"Apple"** is associated with the value **3**.

- To access the value of a dictionary, we use the syntax: **dictName['key']**.

Exercise 21 Correction

```
## Exercise 21
d = {"Apple":15, "Banana":8, "Strawberry":12, "Kiwi":9, "Peach":2}
sum(d.values())
46
```

Comments:

We often need to select the values from a dictionary to use them in our program. In Python, we can do this quickly using the *values()* method, which returns a **dict_values** object that can be converted to a list using the *list()* function.

There's also the *keys()* method to extract only the keys from a dictionary.

Exercise 22 Correction

```
## Exercise 22

float("{:.2f}".format(187.632587))

187.63
```

Comments:

- The Python *format()* function was introduced to efficiently handle complex string formatting. This method works by placing multiple replacement fields defined by pairs of curly braces { } within a string and then calling *string.format(value)*. The parameter passed to the *format()* method corresponds to the value we want to put inside the curly braces of the string.

- It's entirely possible to place multiple curly braces in the same string and pass multiple parameters to the *format()* method.

- In the solution provided for this exercise, we specified the form {:.2f} between the curly braces, which simply means that we will keep **only two digits** after the **decimal point** of the number **187.632587**, which is passed as a parameter.

Exercise 23 Correction

```
## Exercise 23

myName = "Julien"
age = 32
languageName = "Python"

ch = f"My name is {myName} and I am {age} years old. I am learning \
        the language {languageName}".format(myName,age,languageName)
print(ch)
```

My name is Julien and I am 32 years old. I am learning the language Python

Exercise 24 Correction

```
## Exercise 24

for i in range(0,11):
    print("8 x",i,"=",8*i)

8 x 0 = 0
8 x 1 = 8
8 x 2 = 16
8 x 3 = 24
8 x 4 = 32
8 x 5 = 40
8 x 6 = 48
8 x 7 = 56
8 x 8 = 64
8 x 9 = 72
8 x 10 = 80
```

Exercise 25 Correction

```
## Exercise 25

import os

print(os.getcwd())

C:\Users\laurentine.masson
```

Comments:

- The Python **os** module allows performing common operating system-related tasks such as creating directories, deleting files, retrieving folder paths, and more.

- The *getcwd()* function from the *os* module allows us to know the **current working directory path**.

Exercise 26 Correction

```
## Exercise 26

L = [1,2,3,4,5]
## "remove" method to remove element 1
L.remove(1)
L
```

```
[2, 3, 4, 5]
```

Comments:
- The *remove(element)* method allows **removing the element** passed as a parameter **from the list** to which we have applied this method.
Note: This function only removes the first occurrence of the specified element in the list L

Exercise 27 Correction

```
## Exercise 27

import os

file_path = r'C:\Users\laurentine.masson\100_Exercises_python.ipynb'
## retrieve file name i.e 100_Exercises_python.ipynb
file_name = os.path.basename(file_path)
## convert the file name to a list, and retrieve the
## last element of this list which represents the extension
extension_file = file_name.split(".")[-1]
print("File extension :", extension_file)
```

```
File extension : ipynb
```

Comments:

- The *basename(filePath)* function allows us to get the base name from the specified file path as a parameter. This function returns **the base name as a string**.

- The *split(separator)* method allows us to convert a string into a list based on the specified separator character. Here are a few examples:

>> "France is a beautiful country".split(" ") ## the separator here is empty space
["France", "is", "a", "beautiful", "country"]

>> "100_Exercises_python".split(".") ## the exercise example
["100_Exercises_python" , "ipynb"]

Exercise 28 Correction

```
## Exercise 28

import time

## store start time of the program
start = time.time()

###### OUR CODE ###########
for i in range(0,11):
    print("8 x",i,"=",8*i)
############################

## store end time of the program
end = time.time()

## Calculate execution time
print("Code execution time :", end-start)

8 x 0 = 0
8 x 1 = 8
8 x 2 = 16
8 x 3 = 24
8 x 4 = 32
8 x 5 = 40
8 x 6 = 48
8 x 7 = 56
8 x 8 = 64
8 x 9 = 72
8 x 10 = 80
Code execution time : 0.0019137859344482422
```

63

Comments:

- The *time()* function from the **time module** returns the time in seconds since the epoch.
On Windows and most Unix systems, the epoch corresponds to **January 1, 1970, 00:00:00 (UTC).**

Exercise 29 Correction

```
## Exercise 29

import random

L = [3,6,8,7,2,"s","ch","d"]
## randomly mix elements of the L list
random.shuffle(L)

print(L)
```

```
['s', 7, 6, 3, 'ch', 8, 2, 'd']
```

Comments:

- The *shuffle(list)* function from the **random module** allows shuffling the sequence passed as a parameter. Shuffling simply means **changing the positions of the elements within the sequence.**

Exercise 30 Correction

```
## Exercise 30

import random
## choose a random number between 20 and 30
random_number  = random.randint(20,30)
print(random_number)
```

```
30
```

Comments:

The *randint(start, end)* function from the **random module** randomly returns n integer between **20 and 30.**

Exercise 31 Correction

```
## Exercise 31

## 1st loop to define the
## number of lines
for i in range(8):
    ## 2nd loop to display in each line
    ## numbers from 5 to 20
    for j in range(5,21):
        print(j, end = " ")
    ## to return to the line
    print()
```

```
5 6 7 8 9 10 11 12 13 14 15 16 17 18 19 20
5 6 7 8 9 10 11 12 13 14 15 16 17 18 19 20
5 6 7 8 9 10 11 12 13 14 15 16 17 18 19 20
5 6 7 8 9 10 11 12 13 14 15 16 17 18 19 20
5 6 7 8 9 10 11 12 13 14 15 16 17 18 19 20
5 6 7 8 9 10 11 12 13 14 15 16 17 18 19 20
5 6 7 8 9 10 11 12 13 14 15 16 17 18 19 20
5 6 7 8 9 10 11 12 13 14 15 16 17 18 19 20
```

Comments:

- The *print()* function has a parameter **end** qthat allows you to specify the string that will be displayed at the end. By default, **end = "\n"**, , which means that if no value is passed as an argument for **end**, the *print()* function will perform a line break.

- The plain *print()* statement is used to create a line break.

Exercise 32 Correction

```
## Exercise 32

L = [3,6,9,12,15,18,21,24]

## comprehension list
L1 = [l/3 for l in L]
print(L1)
```

```
[1.0, 2.0, 3.0, 4.0, 5.0, 6.0, 7.0, 8.0]
```

Exercise 33 Correction

```
## Exercise 33


L = [-6,5,-3,-1,2,8,-3.6]
## comprehension list
L1 = [l for l in L if l > 0]
print(L1)
```

```
[5, 2, 8]
```

Exercise 34 Correction

```
## Exercise 34

## function definition
## function parameters are:
## a,b et x
def f(a,b,x):
    ## the value returned by our function
    return a*(x**3) + 2*a*(x**2) + b

### ------ Function Call ---- ###
# f(3,0,1)
f(0,2,2)

2
```

┌───┐
Comments:

- In programming, functions are very useful for performing the same operation multiple times with different parameters. They also make the code more readable and clear.

- The functions we have seen so far are built-in functions like **range()**, **len()**, **etc.**

- In Python, **to define a function**, we use the keyword **def**. If we want the function to **return** something, we use the keyword **return**. Here is the **syntax** for defining a function:

*def **FunctionName**(ParameterList):*
    instruction block

    ***return** ...*
└───┘

Exercise 35 Correction

```
## Exercise 35

## Creating a Python function
def CheckPresence(a,L):
    ## if element a is present in L
    if a in L:
        ## then return True
        return True
    ## Otherwise
    else :
        ## returns False
        return False

### ------ Function Call ---- ###
# CheckPresence(2,[1,2,3,4,5,6])
CheckPresence(-1,[3,6,9,7,"abcr"])
```

False

Exercise 36 Correction

```
## Exercise 36

## we take 3018 as an example
number = 3018
## conversion to string
number = str(number)
## Initialize our sum_ variable to 0
sum_ = 0

## iterate through all the elements of our 'number'
for digit in number:
    ## for each digit, convert it to an integer
    ## before adding it to our 'sum_' variable
    sum_ += int(digit)

print(sum_)
```

12

Comments:

- In order to iterate through each digit of the number **3018**, it is necessary to convert this number into a string

Exercise 37 Correction

```
## Exercise 37

def calculateSum(L):
    ## variable initialization
    ## 'sum_' to 0
    sum_ = 0
    ## for each number in the list
    for number in L:
        ## add it to our variable 'sum_'
        sum_ += number

    ## return sum_ of numbers at the
    ## end of the loop
    return sum_

### ------ Function Call ---- ###
# calculateSum([3,2,6,9,-1,5])
calculateSum([-3,-6,0,1,2,7])
```

1

Exercise 38 Correction

```
## Exercise 38

def removeDuplicates(L):
    ## iterate through all the elements of the list L
    for elt in L:
        ## number of occurrences of this
        ## element in the list L
        elt_occ = L.count(elt)
        ## If there are more than two occurrences
        ## of this element in the list L
        if elt_occ >= 2:
            ## delete all occurrences and keep
            ## only one element at the end
            for i in range(elt_occ-1):
                L.remove(elt)
    ## sort the list in ascending order
    L.sort()
    return L

### ------ Function Call ---- ###
# removeDuplicates([0,3,5,7,3,5,1,-1])
removeDuplicates([0,5,9,10,3.2,1,-3])
```

[-3, 0, 1, 3.2, 5, 9, 10]   69

Comments:

- There is another much simpler method to **remove duplicates** from a **list**, which involves converting the **list** into a **set** using the *set()* function. As a result, we obtain a set **containing all the elements without duplication**, which could later be converted back into a list using the *list()* function.

Exercise 39 Correction

```
## Exercise 39

def addElementDict(key,value,d):
    ## add an element
    d[key] = value
    ## return the dictionary d
    ## after adding the element
    return d

### ------ Function Call ---- ###
# addElementDict("baptiste" , 29, {"julien" : 14, "laurent" : 31})
addElementDict("weight" , 65.3, {})

{'weight': 65.3}
```

Exercise 40 Correction

```
## Exercise 40

def maximum(L):
    ## initialize variable max_L with
    ## the first element of the list L
    max_L = L[0]
    ## iterate through all the elements of the list L
    for elt in L:
        ## If the element is greater than the value
        ## stored in max_L
        if elt > max_L:
            ## update variable max_L with this element
            max_L = elt
    ## return the maximum value found
    return max_L

### ------ Function Call ---- ###
# maximum([-9,2,4,1,8])
maximum([-3,1,7,6,2,3])
```

7

Exercise 41 Correction

```
## Exercise 41

def sumSubList(L,i,j):

    ## select the sub-list
    Lij = L[i:j+1]
    ## initialize the variable where
    ## we will store the sum
    sum_ = 0
    ## For each sub-list item
    for elt in Lij:
        ## add this element to the variable sum
        sum_ += elt
    ## return the sum_
    return sum_

### ------ Function Call ---- ###
# sumSubList([4,10,12,16,18], 2, 4)
sumSubList([2,4,6,8,10,12], 0, 2)
```

12

Exercise 42 Correction

```
## Exercise 42

for nbr_star in range(1,11):
    if nbr_star%2 == 0 or nbr_star == 1:
        print("*"*nbr_star)
```

```
*
**
****
******
********
**********
```

Exercise 43 Correction

```
## Exercise 43

def minimum(L):
    ## initialize variable min_L with the
    ## first element of the list L
    min_L = L[0]
    ## iterate through all the elements of the list L
    for elt in L:
        ## If an element of the list is smaller
        ## than the value stored in min_L
        if elt < min_L:
            ## update variable min_L variable
            ## with this new element
            min_L = elt
    ## return the minimum value of L
    return min_L

### ------ Function Call ---- ###
# minimum([-9,2,4,1,8])
minimum([-3,1,7,6,2,3])
```

-3

Exercise 44 Correction

```
## Exercise 44

def length(L):
    ## Initialize list size L to 0
    size_L = 0
    ## iterate through all the elements
    ## of the list L
    for elt in L:
        ## increment variable size_L variable by 1
        ## each time it passes through the loop
        size_L += 1
    ## return the number of elements
    ## existing in list L
    return size_L

### ------ Function Call ---- ###
# length([3,6,7, "abde" , [1,3,57], True])
length([])
```

0

72

Exercise 45 Correction

```
## Exercise 45

def averageList(L):
    ## ---- Calculating the sum of L --- ##
    sum_L = 0
    for elt in L:
        sum_L += elt

    ## calculation of the average
    ## Sum / number_element_L
    average_L = sum_L / len(L)
    ## return the calculated average
    return average_L

### ------ Function Call ---- ###
# averageList([1,2,3,4,5,6,7])
averageList([3,0,-1,5,6,9,17])
```

```
5.571428571428571
```

Comments:

- It is possible to use the *sum(list)* function, which allows obtaining the **sum of the elements** in the parameterized list without using a *for* loop.

Exercise 46 Correction

```
## Exercise 46

def divisor(n):
    ## the list containing the divisors
    n_divisors = []
    ## iterate through all the elements from 1 to n
    for div in range(1,n+1):
        ## if the remainder of the division of n by div is 0
        if n%div == 0:
            ## then div is a divisor of n
            ## and we add it to the list of divisors
            n_divisors.append(div)
    return n_divisors

### ------ Function Call ---- ###
# divisor(3)
divisor(9)
```

```
[1, 3, 9]
```

73

Exercise 47 Correction

```
## Exercise 47

def checkCapitals(sentence):
    ## iterate through all the letters of the
    ## string 'sentence'
    for letter in sentence:
        ## if the letter is capitalized
        if letter.isupper():
            ## return True
            return True
    ## otherwise False
    return False

### ------ Function Call ---- ###
# checkCapitals("Vegetables are good for health")
checkCapitals("this is the best book in python")
```

```
False
```

Comments:

- The method *isupper()* allows checking if a string is in **uppercase**. If the string is in **uppercase**, the method returns **True**; otherwise, it returns **False**.

- There's also the *islower()* method that checks if the string is in **lowercase**.

Exercise 48 Correction

```
## Exercise 48

def concatList(L1,L2,L3):
    ## the + operator is used to
    ## concatenate lists
    L_concat = L1 + L2 + L3
    return L_concat

### ------ Function Call ---- ###
# concatList([0,9,8],[2,6,9],[True,False,"abc"])
concatList([[38,-1],3,-9], ["xz","France"], [])
```

```
[[38, -1], 3, -9, 'xz', 'France']
```

Exercise 49 Correction

```
## Exercise 49

def valueCountDict(d):
    ## extract the list of keys from
    ## the dictionary d
    d_key = list(d.keys())
    ## initialization of the variable that will
    ## hold the number of values in dictionary d
    nbr_value = 0
    ## iterate through all the keys
    for key in d_key:
        ## for each key, determine the number of values
        ## contained in the list associated with that 'key'
        length_val = len(d[key])
        ## add the number of values to the variable nbr_value
        nbr_value += length_val

    return nbr_value

### ------ Function Call ---- ###
# valueCountDict({"a" : [1,2,3], "b" : [3,"p"], "c" : [8]})
valueCountDict({"Julie" : [12,60.1], "Fred" : [26,75.6], "David" : []})
```

4

Exercise 50 Correction

```
## Exercise 50

def concatDict(d1,d2):
    ## concatenation of dictionary
    ## d1 with d2
    d1.update(d2)
    return d1

### ------ Function Call ---- ###
# concatDict({"a":3, "b":6},{"c":2,"d":-1})
concatDict({"d": [2.9,4.1]},{"p" : []})

{'d': [2.9, 4.1], 'p': []}
```

Exercise 51 Correction

```
## Exercise 51

def computeFactorial(n):
    ## factorial of n = nx(n-1)x(n-2)x....*2*1

    ## the factorial of the
    ## number 0 is equal to 1
    if n == 0:
        return 1
    ## the variable that will
    ## contain our final result
    res_factorial = n
    ## run through all elements from n-1 to 1
    for k in range(n-1,0,-1):
        res_factorial = res_factorial*k

    return res_factorial

### ------ Function Call ---- ###
# computeFactorial(0)
# computeFactorial(9)
computeFactorial(3)
```

6

Exercise 52 Correction

```
## Exercise 52

def divisorsMult(n,a,threshold):
    result = []

    ## iterate through the numbers from 0 to threshold
    for nbr in range(threshold+1):
        ## the remainder of the division of nbr by n must equal 0
        ## and the remainder of the division of nbr by a must be different from 0
        if nbr%n == 0 and nbr%a != 0:
            ## if the conditions are satisfied, then
            result.append(nbr)
    return result

### ------ Function Call ---- ###
# divisorsMult(5,2,100)
divisorsMult(11,3,85)

[11, 22, 44, 55, 77]
```

Exercise 53 Correction

```
## Exercise 53

def hasVowel(sentence):
    ## the vowel list
    vowels = ['a','e','i','o','u','y']
    ## iterate through all the vowels
    for v in vowels:
        ## If the vowel exists in the sentence
        ## passed in parameter
        if v in sentence:
            ## return True
            return True
    ## If the sentence contains
    ## no vowel => return False
    return False

### ------ Function Call ---- ###
# hasVowel("I'm going to take my shower")
hasVowel("rbhpm")
```

False

Exercise 54 Correction

```
## Exercise 54

def removeSpaces(sentence):
    ## convert sentence to list
    L_sentence = sentence.split(" ")
    ## convert list back to string
    ## without separator
    sentence_without_space = "".join(L_sentence)

    return sentence_without_space

### ------ Function Call ---- ###
# removeSpaces("France is beautiful!")
removeSpaces("I will take my bike.")
```

'Iwilltakemybike.'

> **Comments:**
>
> - The instruction *separator.join(list)* allows converting a list passed as a parameter into a string by **separating the different elements** of this string with the specified *separator.*

Exercise 55 Correction

```
## Exercise 55

def EltPositionList(L,x):
    ## list of indices for element x
    x_indexes = []
    ## Iterate through all the elements of the list
    for i in range(len(L)):
        ## if an element of L is equal to x
        if L[i] == x:
            ## add its index to the list
            x_indexes.append(i)
    ## if the list is always empty then
    ## element x does not exist in L
    if len(x_indexes) == 0:
        print("Element",x,"is not in list",L)

    ## return the index list of x
    return x_indexes

### ------ Function Call ---- ###
# EltPositionList([1,2,3,6,8,7,3],3)
EltPositionList([6,8,9,1,3,7],-1)
```

Exercise 56 Correction

```
## Exercise 56

def filterWords(sentence,minLength):
    ## convert the sentence into a list using a
    ## a "space" as separator
    sentence_list = sentence.split(" ")
    ## the variable that will contain our phrase
    ## filtered
    sentence_filtered = []
    ## iterate through each element of the list
    for word in sentence_list:
        ## If its length is greater than the minimum
        ## length passed as a parameter
        if len(word) >= minLength:
            ## so we keep this word and add
            ## it to our new list
            sentence_filtered.append(word)

    ## convert the list into a string while keeping
    ## the spaces between the words
    sentence_filtered = " ".join(sentence_filtered)

    return sentence_filtered

### ------ Function Call ---- ###
# filterWords("Hello how are you?",4)
filterWords("Where do you come from?",5)

'Where from?'
```

Exercise 57 Correction

```
## Exercise 57

def reverseSentence(sentence):
    ## convert sentence to list of words
    list_words = sentence.split(" ")
    ## reverse the list of words
    list_words.reverse()
    ## reconstruct the sentence
    ## with spaces between words
    sentence = " ".join(list_words)

    return sentence

### ------ Function Call ---- ###
reverseSentence("could you get me a coffee?")
# reverseSentence("Apple")
```

'coffee? a me get you could'

Exercise 58 Correction

```
## Exercise 58

def occurrenceCount(L):
    ## Initialization of the list in
    ## which we will store our result
    res_tuples = []
    ## iterate through each element of L
    for elt in L:
        ## number of occurrences of the element
        nbrOcc = L.count(elt)
        ## tuple creation (element,NumberOccurrences)
        tup_elt = (elt,nbrOcc)
        ## to avoid duplicate tuples
        ## check if the tuple does not exist in the final result
        if tup_elt not in res_tuples:
            ## if it doesn't exist, add it to the list
            res_tuples.append(tup_elt)
    return res_tuples

### ------ Function Call ---- ###
# occurrenceCount([-4,8,-3,2,1,2,7,9,-3,8,1])
occurrenceCount(["a",3,4,"b","a",3])
```

[('a', 2), (3, 2), (4, 1), ('b', 1)]

Exercise 59 Correction

```python
## Exercise 59

def unionList(L1,L2,L3):
    ## convert all lists into sets
    set1 = set(L1)
    set2 = set(L2)
    set3 = set(L3)

    ## union of the 3 lists
    unionSet = set1 | set2 | set3
    ## convert the union result into a list
    L_union = list(unionSet)
    ## sort the list in order ascending
    L_union.sort()

    return L_union

### ------ Function Call ---- ###
# unionList([3,6,9,3],[1,0,3],[12,6,0])
unionList([7,44,-3],[],[7,2,7])
```

```
[-3, 2, 7, 44]
```

Comments :
- The use of the **|** operator between **sets** signifies the **union of sets** in the mathematical sense.

Exercise 60 Correction

```
## Exercise 60

def calculateGCD(a,b):
    ## check whether the two parameters a and b are positive
    ## if not, return an error
    assert(a>0 and b > 0)
    ## as long as b is not equal to 0
    while b != 0:
        ## double assignment
        ## a is assigned b
        ## b is assigned the remainder of a divided by b
        a,b = b,a%b
    ## return a at the end
    return a

### ------ Function Call ---- ###
# calculateGCD(3,5)
calculateGCD(5,15)
```

5

Exercise 61 Correction

```
## Exercise 61

def readFile(filePath):
    ## open file in read mode
    file = open(filePath,"r")
    ## read file contents
    content = file.read()
    ## close file
    file.close()
    ## return the contents of the file
    return content

# ### ------ Function Call ---- ###
readFile(r"C:\Users\laurentine.masson\Documents\Personal\test.txt")
```

Hello, my name is Gregory and I'm 30 years old.

81

Comments:

- The function *open(filePath, mode)* allows opening a file according to a specified mode. There are several opening modes, including:
r : for reading the file
r+ : for both reading and writing to the file
w : for writing in a file
rb : for reading in binary format
a : for opening a file in append mode
This list is not exhaustive, but for now, these are the main modes you should know.

- The method *read()* allows **reading the content of a file**. This method takes an integer argument that determines the number of characters we want to read. By default, if no number is specified, the method returns all the existing content in the file.

- The method *close()* allows **closing a file** after you're done using it. File closure is essential. Sometimes, certain modifications made to the file do not take effect until the file is closed.

Exercise 62 Correction

```
## Exercise 62

def countOccFile(filePath,word):
    ## open file in read mode
    file = open(filePath,"r")
    ## read all content
    content = file.read()
    ## convert file contents to word list
    list_words = content.split(" ")
    ## initialize the variable storing
    ## the occurrence of the word
    occ_word = 0
    ## iterate through all the words in the list
    for elt in list_words:
        ## if the element in the list is identical
        ## to the searched word
        if elt == word:
            ## increment variable by 1
            occ_word += 1

    return occ_word

### ------ Function Call ---- ###
countOccFile(r"C:\Users\laurentine.masson\Documents\Personal\test.txt", "the")
```

Exercise 63 Correction

```
## Exercise 63

def removeChar(filePath, character):
    ## the use of the syntax 'with open'
    ## automatically closes the file
    with open(filePath, "r") as file:
        content = file.read()

    ## replace the character with a blank
    new_content = content.replace(character,"")

    ## open file in write mode
    with open(filePath, "w") as file:
        ## write new content
        file.write(new_content)

    return

### ------ Function Call ---- ###
removeChar(r"C:\Users\laurentine.masson\Documents\Personal\test.txt",",")
```

Exercise 64 Correction

```
## Exercise 64

def presenceNumber(filePath):
    ## open file in read-only mode
    file = open(filePath, "r")
    ## read the entire contents of the file
    content = file.read()
    ## iterate through each character of the file
    for c in content:
        ## Check if a character is a number
        if c.isdigit():
            return True
    return False

### ------ Function Call ---- ###
presenceNumber(r"C:\Users\laurentine.masson\Documents\Personal\test.txt")
## the test.txt file does not contain a number
```

```
False
```

Exercise 65 Correction

```
## Exercise 65

import os

def fileCount(folderPath):
    ## counter initialization
    nbr_file = 0
    ## list all folder contents
    listing_content = os.listdir(folderPath)
    ## iterate through the contents of the folder
    for content in listing_content:
        ## if the content is a file
        if os.path.isfile(os.path.join(folderPath,content)):
            ## increment variable nbr_file
            nbr_file += 1
    return nbr_file

### ------ Function Call ---- ###
fileCount(r"C:\Users\fileCount\Documents\Personal")
```

5

Comments:

- The function *listdir(path)* from the **os** module allows obtaining the **list** of **all files** and **directories** in the specified path.

- The function *os.path.join(path1, path2, ..)* intelligently combines one or more path components. This method concatenates multiple paths using exactly one directory separator " / ".

- The function *os.path.isfile(path)* allows checking if the path provided as a parameter indeed corresponds to a file.

Exercise 66 Correction

```python
## Exercise 66

def writeFile(fileName,text):
    ## open a file in write mode
    f = open(fileName, "w")
    ## writing the text provided as a parameter
    ## into the file
    f.write(text)
    ## close file
    f.close()

### ------ Function Call ---- ###
myPath = r"C:\Users\laurentine.masson\Documents\Personal\test.txt"
myText = "I study at the Henri IV school"
writeFile(myPath,myText)
```

Exercise 67 Correction

```python
## Exercise 67

def maxKeyUniqueValuesDict(d):
    key_val = []
    ## dictionary key listing
    d_keys = list(d.keys())
    ## iterate through all the keys of the dictionary
    for key in d_keys:
        ## the number of values associated with the key
        ## without counting duplicates
        nbr_val_unique = len(set(d[key]))
        ## add tuple (key, number of unique values)
        ## in the list
        key_val.append((key,nbr_val_unique))

    ## sort by 2nd tuple element
    key_val.sort(key = lambda x : x[1])
    ## extract the key with the maximum number of values
    key_max_val = key_val[-1][0]

    return key_max_val

### ------ Function Call ---- ###
# maxKeyUniqueValuesDict({"a" : [9,10,9,7,3,1], "b" : [5,3,2,2,2], "c" : [1,1,1,1,1,1,8,2]})
maxKeyUniqueValuesDict({"dtg" : [6,8,1], "fgb" : [2.5, "a"], "klm" : ["p" ,3,3]})

'dtg'
```

85

Exercise 68 Correction

```python
## Exercise 68

user_list = []

##request the number of items the list must contain
nbr_element = int(input("Enter the number of items in the list: "))
## ask for as many numbers as the list should contain
for i in range(nbr_element):
    elt = int(input("Enter an item from the list:"))
    ## add this item to the list
    user_list.append(elt)

print(user_list)
```

```
Enter the number of items in the list: 4
Enter an item from the list:8
Enter an item from the list:7
Enter an item from the list:0
Enter an item from the list:3
[8, 7, 0, 3]
```

Exercise 69 Correction

```python
## Exercise 69

from datetime import datetime

def daysHoursCount(startDate,endDate):
    ## date format
    date_format = "%Y/%m/%d"
    ## convert string start date to date format
    date_start_format = datetime.strptime(startDate,date_format)
    ## convert string end date to date format
    date_end_format = datetime.strptime(endDate,date_format)
    ## number of days between start date and end date
    nbrDays = (date_end_format - date_start_format).days
    ## calculating the number of hours
    nbrHours = nbrDays * 24

    return nbrDays,nbrHours

### ------ Function Call ---- ###
# daysHoursCount("2022/05/15","2022/06/20")
daysHoursCount("2022/04/1","2022/04/27")
```

```
(26, 624)
```

86

Comments:

- The parameters passed to the function are of **string type**. Therefore, it's necessary to convert these parameters into **date format** in order to calculate the **number of days** between the start date and the end date.

- The function ***datetime.strptime(date,formatDate)*** allows converting the **string date** into **datetime** format using the specified **formatDate**.

Exercise 70 Correction

```python
## Exercise 70

## Importing modules
import string
import random
## creation of a list of characters from which
## we'll randomly generate our password
list_characters = list(string.ascii_letters + string.digits + "!@#$%^&*()")

def generatePassword(characters, passwordLength):
    ## randomly mix characters
    random.shuffle(characters)
    ## create a list containing our password
    password = []
    ## randomly select password characters
    ## until the size specified in parameters is reached
    for i in range(passwordLength):
        charac_rand = random.choice(characters)
        ## add the randomly chosen character
        ## in the password list
        password.append(charac_rand)

    ## mix our list again which will contain our password
    random.shuffle(password)
    ## convert list to string
    ## without spaces between characters
    password = "".join(password)

    return password

### ------ Function Call ---- ###
generatePassword(list_characters,10)
```

'0P96w#m3Cd'

87

Comments :

- The character list from which we generated our password includes **alphabetical letters** from **A to Z** in both **lowercase** and **uppercase**, **digits** from **0 to 9**, and some **special characters**.
The **string** module provides us the ability to obtain the string containing all letters and digits by concatenating the results of **string.ascii_letters** and **string.digits**.

Exercise 71 Correction

```
## Exercise 71

## module import
import math

def trigoFunct(x):
    ## definition of the function to be calculated
    f = math.cos(x)*math.sin(x) + math.sin(x) + 8

    return f

### ------ Function Call ---- ###
# trigoFunct(math.pi/4)
trigoFunct(math.pi)
```

```
8.0
```

Comments:

- The **math** module contains several mathematical functions that are already available in Python. This can be useful when we need to use complex statistical functions, trigonometric functions, and so on.

Exercise 72 Correction

```python
## Exercise 72

int_list = []

## iterate through all the numbers
## between 100 and 999
for nbr in range(100,1000):
    ## convert the number into a string
    str_nbr = str(nbr)
    ## sum the digits of the number
    sum_digits = int(str_nbr[0]) + int(str_nbr[1]) + int(str_nbr[2])
    ## multiply the digits of the number
    multi_digits = int(str_nbr[0])*int(str_nbr[1])*int(str_nbr[2])
    ## if the remainder of the division of multi_digits
    ## by sum_digits is equal to 0
    if multi_digits%sum_digits == 0:
        ## then add the number to the list of integers
        int_list.append(nbr)

print(int_list)
```

Exercise 73 Correction

```python
## Exercise 73

def calculateSum(L):
    ## if the list is empty
    if len(L) == 0: ## or if not L
        ## return 0
        return 0
    ## otherwise calculate the
    ## sum using recursion
    return L[0] + calculateSum(L[1:])

### ------ Function Call ---- ###
# calculateSum([3,2,6,9,-1,5])
calculateSum([-3,-6,0,1,2,7])
```

1

> **Comments :**
>
> - The use of **recursive** functions is very helpful in cases where the **calculatio‹**
> **is repetitive.** As a reminder, a recursive function is a function that contains a**t**
> least one call to itself. For example, we can use recursion in calculating the
> **power of a number, calculating the factorial,** etc.

Exercise 74 Correction

```
## Exercise 74

def fibonacciSequence(N):
    ## if the number N passed in parameter
    ## is less than or equal to 2
    if N <= 2:
        ## the result of the sequence is 1
        return 1
    ## otherwise call the same function using recursion
    return fibonacciSequence(N-1) + fibonacciSequence(N-2)

### ------ Function Call ---- ###
# fibonacciSequence(25)
fibonacciSequence(45)
```

```
1134903170
```

Exercise 75 Correction

```
## Exercise 75

def isEven(N):
    ## if the number passed as parameter is equal to 1
    if N == 1:
        ## then it is not even
        return False
    ## otherwise call up the isOdd(N-1) function
    return isOdd(N-1)


def isOdd(N):
    ## if the number passed as
    ## parameter is equal to 1
    if N == 1:
        ## then N is odd
        return True
    ## otherwise, call the function isEven in N-1
    return isEven(N-1)

### ------ Function Call ---- ###
# isEven(5)
isOdd(7)
```

True

Comments :

- **Recursion** is **mutual** *(or cross)* when a function *func1()* calls another function *func2()* that triggers a recursive call to *func1()*. The situation is necessarily symmetrical, as *func2()* will trigger a call to *func1()*, which in turn will trigger a call to *func1()*

Exercise 76 Correction

```
## Exercise 76

def join(L,character):
    ## initialize a string empty
    str_charac = ""
    ## iterate through all the indices of the elements in L
    for i in range(len(L)):
        ## add the element from L located at index i to the string
        ## str_charac
        str_charac += L[i]
        ## if not the last element we add
        ## the separator character
        if i != len(L)-1:
            str_charac += character
    ## return the string obtained from L using the
    ## separator passed as parameters
    return str_charac

### ------ Function Call ---- ###
# join(["Hello","Aurélie"]," ")
join(["Hi"," How are you?"], ",")
```

'Hi, How are you?'

Exercise 77 Correction

```
## Exercise 77

def replaceString(sentence,oldWord,newWord):
    ## if the word we want to replace exists
    ## in the sentence passed as parameters
    if oldWord in sentence:
        ## extract the beginning index from the old word
        start_oldWord_idx = sentence.index(oldWord)
        ## extract the end index of from old word
        end_oldWord_idx = start_oldWord_idx + len(oldWord)
        ## convert the sentence to character list
        sentence_list = list(sentence)
        ## replace the old word with the new one
        sentence_list[start_oldWord_idx:end_oldWord_idx] = newWord
        ## reconstitute the new sentence by
        ## converting the list into a string
        sentence = "".join(sentence_list)
    return sentence

### ------ Function Call ---- ###
# replaceString("Hello Aurélie","Aurélie","Mathilde")
replaceString("I'm 50 years old", "50","35")
```

"I'm 35 years old"

Exercise 78 Correction

```
## Exercice 78

def split(sentence,character):
    ## the variable that will contain our list
    sentence_list = []
    ## initialization of a temporary variable
    word_tmp = ""
    ## if the character is in the phrase passed in parameters
    if character in sentence:
        ## iterate through all the indices of
        ## the elements in the sentence
        for i in range(len(sentence)):
            ## as long as the element in the index is
            ## different from the "character" separator
            if sentence[i] != character:
                ## then we concatenate this element
                ## with our temporary variable
                word_tmp += sentence[i]
                ## if i is equal to the index of the last element
                if i == len(sentence)-1:
                    ## add the last word
                    sentence_list += [word_tmp]
            ## if the element at index i is equal to the separator
            else:
                ## then add the temporary word to our list
                sentence_list += [word_tmp]
                ## and reset the temporary word
                word_tmp = ""
        return sentence_list
    # if the separator does not exist in the sentence
    else:
        ## then add the whole sentence to the list
        sentence_list += [sentence]
        return sentence_list

### ------ Function Call ---- ###
# split("Hello Aurélie", " ")
split("Hi, how are you?", ",")

['Hi', ' how are you?']
```

Exercise 79 Correction

```
## Exercise 79

def isdigit(string):
    ## number lists
    numbers = ['0','1','2','3','4','5','6','7','8','9']
    ## iterate through all the elements of the string
    for c in string:
        ## if character c does not exist in the numbers list
        if c not in numbers:
            ## return False
            return False
    ## otherwise return True
    return True

### ------ Function Call ---- ###
# isdigit("125920")
isdigit("edgte9be")
```

False

Exercise 80 Correction

```
## Exercise 80

def isPalindrome(nbr):
    ## if the number passed in parameters
    ## is less than or equal to 10
    if nbr <= 10:
        ## then it's not a palindrome
        return False
    ## if greater than 10
    else:
        ## convert to string
        nbr_str = str(nbr)
        ## take its reverse
        nbr_str_reverse = nbr_str[::-1]
        ## check whether the number and its reverse are equal
        if nbr_str == nbr_str_reverse:
            ## return True
            return True

### ------ Function Call ---- ###
# isPalindrome(10)
isPalindrome(919)
```

True

Exercise 81 Correction

```
## Exercise 81

## list where we'll store the numbers found
palindrome_numbers = []
## Two loops from 100 to 999 to cover
## all possible cases
for i in range(100,1000):
    for j in range(100,1000):
        ## multiply those two numbers
        nbr = i*j
        ## if the result is a palindrome number
        if isPalindrome(nbr):
            ## add it to the list
            palindrome_numbers.append(nbr)

## The largest number of palindromes in our list is
largest_palindrome = max(palindrome_numbers)
print(largest_palindrome)
```

```
906609
```

Exercise 82 Correction

```
## Exercise 82
import math

def isPrime(number):
    ## the divisor must be greater than or equal to 2,
    ## so we initialize it to 2
    divisor = 2
    ## as long as the divisor does not exceed the square root of "number"
    while divisor <= math.sqrt(number):
        ## if "number" is divisible by d then
        if number%divisor == 0:
            ## a divisor is found and "number" is not prime
            return False
        divisor += 1
    ## if no divisor is found, then "number" is prime
    return True

def isCircularPrime(number):

    ## if, for example, the input parameter is "number = 197"
    ## then this list will contain 197,971 and 719
    circular_number = []

    ## convert number to string
    number = str(number)
    ## Find all circular numbers of the input parameter 'number'.
    for i in range(len(number)):
        circular_number.append(number[i:] + number[:i])

    ## Test if all numbers in the 'circular_number' list are circular
    prime_circular = True
    for num in circular_number:
        ## convert "num" from string to integer
        num = int(num)
        ## you can use the isPrime(nbr) function
        if not isPrime(num):
            ## if only one number is not prime then the 'number' given
            ## as a parameter is not circular prime
            prime_circular = False
    return prime_circular

### ------ Function Call ---- ###
# isCircularPrime(9377)
isCircularPrime(36)
```

```
False
```

95

Exercise 83 Correction

```
## Exercise 83

def isDistinct(number):
    ## convert number to type string
    nbr_str = str(number)
    ## iterate through each digit of the number
    for digit in nbr_str:
        ## if the digit exists more than once in the number
        if nbr_str.count(digit) >= 2:
            ## return False
            return False
    ## otherwise return True
    return True

### ------ Function Call ---- ###
# isDistinct(9647)
isDistinct(1343)
```

False

Exercise 84 Correction

```
## Exercise 84

def codeSum(number):

    assert(number >= 100)

    sum_digit = 0
    nbr_str = str(number)
    compute_sum = True


    while compute_sum:
        for nbr in nbr_str:
            sum_digit += int(nbr)

        if sum_digit <= 9 and sum_digit >=1:
            compute_sum = False

        else:
            nbr_str = str(sum_digit)
            sum_digit = 0


    final_code = int(str(sum_digit) + str(number))

    return final_code

### ------ Function Call ---- ###
codeSum(69810)
# codeSum(3201)
```

669810

Exercise 85 Correction

```
## Exercise 85

def dichotomicSearch(L,elt):

    ## sort list in ascending order
    L.sort()
    ## as long as the list is not empty
    while L:
        ## middle index
        idx_middle = len(L) // 2
        ## If the middle element is equal to the target element
        if elt == L[idx_middle]:
            ## return True
            return True
        ## If the target element is smaller than
        ## the element in the middle of L
        elif elt < L[idx_middle]:
            ## Keep only the elements whose index
            ## is smaller than idx_middle
            L = L[:idx_middle]
        ## If the target element is greater than the
        ## element in the middle of L
        else:
            ## Keep only the elements whose index
            ## is greater than idx_middle
            L = L[idx_middle+1:]
    ## if no element is found, then
    return False

### ------ Function Call ---- ###
# dichotomicSearch([6,9,15,36,41,43,47],41)
dichotomicSearch([-9,-1,3,4,7,11],0)
```

```
False
```

Exercise 86 Correction

```
## Exercise 86

## 3 for loops to cover all possible
## cases of the triplet (x, y, z)
for x in range(1,1000):
    for y in range(x+1,1000):
        for z in range(y+1,1000):
            ## if both equations are verified
            if x**2 + y**2 == z**2:
                if x+y+z == 1000:
                    ## display the numbers x,y,z
                    ## and their products
                    print("x =", x)
                    print("y =", y)
                    print("z =", z)
                    print("x*y*z =",x*y*z)
```

```
x = 200
y = 375
z = 425
x*y*z = 31875000
```

97

Exercise 87 Correction

```
## Exercise 87

def processFile(filePath):
    ## open the first file in read mode
    with open(filePath, "r") as file1:
        ## open the second file in write mode
        with open("test2.txt", "w") as file2:
            ## for each line in file1
            for line in file1:
                ## remove line breaks when writing to the new file
                file2.write(line.rstrip("\n"))

### ------ Function Call ---- ###
processFile(r"C:\Users\laurentine.masson\Documents\Personal\test.txt")
```

Exercise 88 Correction

```
## Exercise 88

def ascendingSort(L):
    ## iterate through all the indexes of the list L
    for i in range(len(L)):
        ## for all indexes greater than i
        for j in range(i+1, len(L)):
            ## if the element at index i is greater than the element at j
            if L[i] > L[j]:
                ## exchange the location of these two numbers
                L[i], L[j] = L[j], L[i]
    return L

### ------ Function Call ---- ###
# ascendingSort([6,1,9,-6,1,8,7])
ascendingSort([-3,5.3,2,7,1,2.3,9.5])

[-3, 1, 2, 2.3, 5.3, 7, 9.5]
```

Exercise 89 Correction

```
## Exercise 89

## Define Person class
class Person:
    ## constructor init
    def __init__(self,height,weight,age):
        ## class attributes
        self.height = height
        self.weight = weight
        self.age = age

    ## 1st class method
    def calculateBMI(self):
        ## BMI calculation formula
        return self.weight / (self.height**2)
    ## 2nd method of the class
    def interpretBMI(self):
        ## Display according to BMI calculation
        if self.calculateBMI() <= 18.5:
            return "The BMI calculation indicates that the person is underweight (thinness)"

        elif self.calculateBMI() >= 30:
            return "The person is obese"

        else:
            return "The person is overweight or has a normal body weight"

## --- Instance creation + use of methods --- ##
julien = Person(1.87,95,26) ## --> Creating an instance (or object) of the Person class
print(julien.calculateBMI()) ## --> Calling an instance method
print(julien.interpretBMI()) ## --> Calling another instance method
```

```
27.166919271354622
The person is overweight or has a normal body weight
```

Comments:

- In programming, the concept of a class allows us to generalize the notion of « type » in order to create **new data structures**.
A class defines attributes and methods. In the case of this exercise, the class **Person** will be used to **create objects** that represent **individuals**.
This class will be able to define attributes such as height, weight and age.
These attributes correspond to properties that characterize an individual, and consequently, they can be used in methods like *calculateBMI()* and *interpretBMI()*.

- If, during the creation of an object, we want certain actions to be performed *(such as initializing attributes)*, we can use a **constructor**.

- A **constructor** is a method, with no **return value**, that has a name imposed by the Python language: **_init_()**. This method is **automatically called** when the object is created. The constructor can have any number of parameters, possibly **none**.

- You may have noticed the use of the word **self**. In fact, **self** is used to represent the instance of our class! It's thanks to **"self"** that we can access the **attributes** and **methods** of our class.
By using **self** before the attributes **height**, **weight** and **age**, we indicate that these attributes are **instance variables**, meaning **they change from one object to another.**
Similarly, for **methods,** indicating **self** as a parameter signifies that they are **instance methods,** meaning we can call these methods on any **instances** *(or objects)* that we create.

- It's impossible to directly modify the data of an object. In fact, it's not possible to directly manipulate the data of an object; it's necessary to go through its methods, which act as a mandatory interface. This is called **encapsulation**, which is a very useful concept in **object-oriented** programming.

- If we want to **modify the attributes** of an object, we need to create **what are called mutators** *(class methods that allow us to modify attributes).*

Note:

- Inside a class, we no longer refer to **functions** but to **methods.**

Exercise 90 Correction

```
## Exercise 90

class Rectangle:
    ## constructor to automatically initialize
    ## the instance to be created
    def __init__(self,width,length):
        self.width = width
        self.length = length

    ## method for calculating the perimeter
    ## of a rectangle
    def Perimeter(self):
        return 2*(self.width+self.length)
    ## method for calculating the area of a rectangle
    def Area(self):
        return self.width * self.length


## create an instance of the Rectangle class
rectangle1 = Rectangle(10,15)
## display rectangle1 width
print("The width of rectangle1 is:", rectangle1.width)
## display length of rectangle1
print("The length of rectangle1 is:",rectangle1.length)
## calculate the perimeter of the rectangle1
print("The perimeter of rectangle1 is: ",rectangle1.Perimeter())
## calculate the area of rectangle1
print("The area of rectangle1 is: ",rectangle1.Area())

The width of rectangle1 is: 10
The length of rectangle1 is: 15
The perimeter of rectangle1 is:  50
calculate the area of rectangle1:  150
```

Exercise 91 Correction

```
## Exercise 91

## definition of a class that inherits
## another class
class Parallelepiped(Rectangle):
    ## Python constructor
    def __init__(self,width,length,height):
        ## Initialization of Parent class attributes
        Rectangle.__init__(self,width,length)
        ## new Parallelepiped class attribute
        self.height = height
    ## method that calculates volume
    def Volume(self):
        return self.length*self.width*self.height

## creating an instance of the Parallelepiped class
parallelepiped1 = Parallelepiped(9,5,2)
## calculating the perimeter of the parallelepiped
print("Perimeter of the parallelepiped1: ", parallelepiped1.Perimeter())
## volume calculation
print("Volume of the parallelepiped1: ", parallelepiped1.Volume())

Perimeter of the parallelepiped1:  28
Volume of the parallelepiped1:  90
```
101

Comments:

- In object-oriented programming, the concept of **class inheritance** is very important. When we say that a class *(child class)* inherits from another class *(parent class)*, the child class **has access to all the attributes and methods of** the parent class.

- In the case of this exercise, the **Parallelepiped** class inherits from the **Rectangle class**. Consequently, any instance of the **Parallelepiped** class has access to the attributes of the **Rectangle**, namely *length* and *width*, as well as the methods *"Perimeter"* and *"Surface."*

Exercise 92 Correction

```
## Exercise 92

class BankAccount:
    ## attribute initialization constructor
    def __init__(self, name = "Maxime", balance = 600):
        self.name = name
        self.balance = balance

    ## deposit method
    def deposit(self,amount):
        self.balance += amount
    ## withdraw method
    def withdraw(self,amount):
        self.balance -= amount
    ## special method
    def __repr__(self):
        return "The balance of " + self.name + "'s bank account is " + str(self.balance) + " euros."
## -- Creating instances and calling methods -- ##
account1 = BankAccount("Julie",1000)
account1.deposit(400)
account1.withdraw(100)
account1

account2 = BankAccount()
account2.deposit(500)
account2
```

```
The balance of Maxime's bank account is 1100 euros.
```

Comments:

- The method **_repr_()** is a **special method** used within a class to represent an object of a class as a string. This method can be used to generate and define your **custom string representation** of objects from a class. For example, in this exercise, by writing the instance name **"account2"** in the console we obtain the **display defined in this special method.**

Exercise 93 Correction

```
## Exercise 93

class Car:
    ## attribute initialization constructor with default attributes
    def __init__(self,brand="peugeot",color="noir",driverName="Aucun",startingKm=16900):
        self.brand = brand
        self.color = color
        self.driverName = driverName
        self.startingKm = startingKm
    ## driver change method
    def chooseDriver(self,driverName):
        self.driverName = driverName
        return self.driverName
    ## circulation distance calculation method
    def calculateDistance(self,finalKm):
        distance_traveled = finalKm - self.startingKm
        return distance_traveled
    ## display information
    def displayInfo(self):
        currentKm = self.calculateDistance(20000) + self.startingKm
        return "The " + self.color + " " + self.brand + " car driven by " + self.driverName + \
        " currently has a mileage of " + str(currentKm) + " km"

## -- Creating instances and calling methods -- ##
car1 = Car()
print("Driver change: ", car1.chooseDriver("Patrick"))
print("Circulation distance: ", car1.calculateDistance(20000))
car1.displayInfo()

Driver change:  Patrick
Circulation distance:  3100

'The noir peugeot car driven by Patrick currently has a mileage of 20000 km'
```

Exercise 94 Correction

```
## Exercise 94

class Point2D:
    ## Initialization constructor attributes
    def __init__(self,x,y):
        self.x = x
        self.y = y
    ## Operator overload +
    def __add__(self,p):
        return self.x + p.x, self.y + p.y
    ## Operator overload -
    def __sub__(self,p):
        return self.x - p.x, self.y - p.y
    ## Operator overload x
    def __mul__(self,p):
        return self.x * p.x, self.y * p.y
    ## Operator overload /
    def __truediv__(self,p):
        return self.x/p.x, self.y/p.y

## -- Creating instances and calling methods -- ##
p1 = Point2D(3,2)
p2 = Point2D(1,4)
print("p1-p2 =",p1-p2)
print("p1+p2 =",p1+p2)
print("p1/p2 =",p1/p2)

p1-p2 = (2, -2)
p1+p2 = (4, 6)
p1/p2 = (3.0, 0.5)
```

103

> **Comments:**
> - **Operator overloading** allows us to redefine an operator within a class. The purpose of **operator overloading** is to redefine operators like **addition, multiplication, division, representation,** etc. in a Python class.
>
> - For instance, in Python, the « **+** » operator is **overloaded** by the **int** and **str** classes. Therefore, we can perform standard addition between two integers: **4+10** results in **14,** and we can also concatenate two strings: **"he" + "llo"** yields **"hello"**
>
> - In the context of this exercise, we aim to perform operations like **addition** *(multiplication, division, etc.)* on **two two-dimensional points**, which are instances of the **Point2D** class. Hence, **overloading** the various used **operators** is necessary.

Exercise 95 Correction

```python
## Exercise 95

class ComplexNumber:
    ## Initialization constructor attributes
    def __init__(self,real,img):
        self.real = real
        self.img = img

    ## representation overload
    def __str__(self):
        return str(self.real) + " " + " " + str(self.img) + "i"
    ## representation overload
    def __repr__(self):
        return str(self.real) + " " + " " + str(self.img) + "i"

## -- Creating instances and calling methods -- ##
nbr1 = ComplexNumber(2,7)
## Display result from overloading using __str__() method
print(nbr1)
## Display result from overloading using __repr__() method
nbr1

2 + 7i

2 + 7i
```

104

Comments:

- The special method __str__() allows you to specify the string representation of an object. This string is returned when using the str() function on an object or when using the print() function.

- If the special method __str__() is not defined in the class, then the __repr__() method will be used instead.

Exercise 96 Correction

```
## Exercise 96

class CustomList:
    ## Initialization constructor of a list
    def __init__(self,*numbers):
        self.numbers = []
        for number in numbers:
            if type(number) == int or type(number) == float:
                self.numbers.append(number)
            else:
                print(f"Operation not allowed: it is not possible to initialize the list with {number}")
    ## append() method
    def append(self,number):
        ## whether the number is an integer or a decimal
        if type(number) == int or type(number) == float:
            ## then add this number to the list
            if number not in self.numbers:
                self.numbers.append(number)
            else:
                return f"The number {number} already exists in the list {self}"
        ## If the number is not an integer or a decimal,
        ## return the following sentence
        else:
            return f"Forbidden operation: It is not possible to add type {type(number)} to the list"

    ## representation overload
    def __repr__(self):
        return f"{self.numbers}"
    ## representation overload
    def __str__(self):
        return f"{self.numbers}"

## -- Creating instances and calling methods -- ##
L1 = CustomList(5,2,3,7,9)
print(L1)
L1.append(2)
L1.append("abc")
L1.append(10)
print(L1)

[5, 2, 3, 7, 9]
[5, 2, 3, 7, 9, 10]
```

Exercise 97 Correction

```
## Exercise 97

import string
## Listing of all digits from 0 to 9 + addition of comma
## and period characters.
character_list = list(string.digits) + [",",".","."]
class customString:
    ## Initialization constructor
    def __init__(self,string):
        list_str = list(string)
        for c in list_str:
            if c in character_list:
                print("The created instance should only contain alphabetical letters")
                print(f"The character \"{c}\" will be removed")
                string = string.replace(c,"")
        self.string = string

    def __add__(self,new_string):
        if new_string in character_list:
            return f"You cannot add \"{new_string}\" to the string"
        else:
            self.string += new_string

        return self.string

    def __repr__(self):
        return self.string

## -- Creating instances and calling methods -- ##
string1 = customString("He,llo")
string1 + ","
string1 + "."
string2 = string1 + " How are you?"
string2
```

```
The created instance should only contain alphabetical letters
The character "," will be removed

'Hello How are you?'
```

Exercise 98 Correction

```
## Exercise 98

def orderDict(d):
    ## list that will contain the tuples
    list_tuples = []
    ## list of dictionary keys
    key_d = list(d.keys())
    ## list of values
    values_d = list(d.values())
    ## loop over (key,value)
    for key,value in zip(key_d,values_d):
        ## add tuple to list
        list_tuples.append((key,value))
    ## order in ascending order as follows
    ## the first element of the tuple
    list_tuples.sort(key = lambda x : x[0])
    ## return a dictionary
    return dict(list_tuples)

## -- Function call -- ##
# orderDict({"a":1,"d" : 7, "b" : 3, "c" : 2})
orderDict({8:9,2:3,9:11})
```

```
{2: 3, 8: 9, 9: 11}
```

106

Comments:

In Python versions **before 3.7**, dictionaries are **not ordered.** This means that even if you sort the dictionary, you cannot store it in a way that preserves the order.

In **Python 3.7** and later versions, **the order of a dictionary is the same as the order of insertion**. So, when you sort the dictionary, the order of its elements will **remain the same when stored.**

The **zip** function is a Python function that takes **two** or **more sequences** and returns a **list of tuples** where each tuple contains an element from each sequence.

Exercise 99 Correction

```
## Exercise 99

## sum sub-sequence of list
def sumSubSeq(L,i,j):
    Lij = L[i:j+1]
    return sum(Lij)


def largestSum(L):
    ## initialization of a variable 'sum_max'
    ## with the first element of the list L
    sum_max = L[0]
    ## Loop through all the indexes of L
    for i in range(len(L)):
        ## Loop through the indexes of L starting from i
        for j in range(i, len(L)):
            ## Call the function to sum the sequence from i to j
            s = sumSubSeq(L, i, j)
            ## If the sum found is greater than the one we initialized
            if s > sum_max :
                ## Store the found sequence in a variable 'seq'
                seq = L[i:j+1]
                ## Change the content of sum_max with the content
                ## of the new variable s
                sum_max = s

    return sum_max,seq

## -- Function call -- ##
# largestSum([-8,-4,6,8,-6,10,-4,-4])
largestSum([-6,1,8,-7,1,9,-1,2])

(13, [1, 8, -7, 1, 9, -1, 2])
```

Exercise 100 Correction

```
## Exercise 100

def separateElements(L):
    ## number of 0's in L
    nbr_0 = L.count(0)
    ## number of 1's in L
    nbr_1 = L.count(1)
    ## create a new list with the same numbers
    L1 = [0]*nbr_0 + [1]*nbr_1
    return L1

## -- Function call -- ##
# separateElements([1, 0, 1, 0, 1, 0, 1, 0])
separateElements([1,0,0,0,1,0,1,1,1,0,1,1,0,0,0,1])
```

[0, 0, 0, 0, 0, 0, 0, 0, 1, 1, 1, 1, 1, 1, 1, 1]

Note : The table below will help you gather all the commands and functions that you find useful and are frequently used, which will greatly aid your learning.

For each command or function, I encourage you to write their syntax along with a simple example that will help you remember their use cases.

You can draw inspiration from the various corrected exercises and previous course reminders.

Command	Functions	Syntax / Minimal example

Command	Functions	Syntax / Minimal example

Command	Functions	Syntax / Minimal example

Printed in Great Britain
by Amazon